For those who long to have the kind of faith that can weather the worst circumstances, Michele Cushatt has written a practical and deeply encouraging guide that will meet them right where they are. Whether you're wrestling with hard questions, enduring a tough season, or simply want to deepen your confidence in a God who sees you and is for you, this is a go-to resource. You will not only gain new insights and renewed strength but discover that Michele is that friend who gets it.

—ALLI WORTHINGTON, author, *Standing Strong*
and *Remaining You While Raising Them*

In *A Faith That Will Not Fail*, we discover Michele Cushatt's heart for God, for His Word, and for His people shining on every page. Her wisdom is hard earned and her experiences resonate. The ten spiritual practices she walks us through are deeply practical and desperately needed. In the midst of our hurry-up culture, Michele calls us to lament, let go, be content, be at peace. A beautiful and timely resource.

—LIZ CURTIS HIGGS, bestselling author, *Bad Girls of the Bible*

A Faith That Will Not Fail does more than it promises, offering practical wisdom for building a faith that not only survives but thrives in difficult seasons. This is a must-read for anyone wanting to stay in love—and on mission—with Jesus when storm clouds gather.

—CRAIG A. SMITH, PhD, lead pastor, Mission Hills Church; author,
How (Not) to Miss God Moving and *The Kingdom for the Kingless*

We become more like Jesus when we practice what He practiced. Michele Cushatt weaves deeply relatable stories with foundational truths of spiritual practices we can all adopt as our own. As a wise woman who threads her story into the needle of life, Michele stitches together a helpful pattern for how to live out a faith that will not fail. I highly recommend this book.

—ELISA MORGAN, author, *You Are Not Alone*; cohost, *Discover the Word* and *God Hears Her*; president emerita, MOPS International

This devotional is unlike any I have read. It is not pithy encouragement for the distracted Christian. Rather, it is a gritty journey of clinging to God for those whose hearts have been ravished by pain and doubt. Michele tells the truth because she is living it. She is a Hebrews 11 woman in our time. "By faith" will you join her?

—JULI SLATTERY, coauthor, *Surprised by the Healer*;
president and cofounder, Authentic Intimacy

If you find yourself wanting a faith that can withstand the inevitable storms of life, this beautiful book is for you. Respected Christian thinker and author Michele Cushatt delivers an accessible, honest guide toward an enduring faith, but without leaning on easy, cliched answers. In *A Faith That Will Not Fail*, Michelle offers ten ancient (and sometimes surprising) practices that will help you go the distance.

—JENNIFER DUKES LEE, author, *Growing Slow*
and *It's All under Control*

Master storyteller Michele Cushatt weaves true-life experiences with biblical insights and wisdom from trusted Christian voices to guide us through ten powerful, life-shaping practices, from humility and lament to contentment and connection. *A Faith That Will Not Fail* is one of those rare books you will want to read, savor, gift, and return to again and again.

—JODIE BERNDT, bestselling author, *Praying
the Scriptures for Your Children*

I've learned over the past few years that God absolutely wants to use suffering to build up our faith. I've also learned that having a friend who understands my questions, cries, and confusion is a rare gift. In *A Faith That Will Not Fail*, Michele Cushatt invites us to witness her faith-building journey—not to impress us but to remind us that we are not alone. Life-giving and practical, my dog-eared, marked, and tearstained copy has gained a permanent spot among other time-honored favorites.

—STACEY THACKER, author, *Threadbare Prayer: Prayers
for Hearts That Feel Hidden, Hurt, and Hopeless*

Even though we often try to simulate faith through determination and white-knuckling, *A Faith That Will Not Fail* reminds us that true faith is found in the low places. Michele gently leads us to counterintuitive practices that loosen our grip, bringing us to weakness and surrender, the path where God gifts faith.

—AMY CARROLL, international speaker; author, *Exhale* and *Esther: Seeing Our Invisible God in an Uncertain World*

I remember going through Blackaby's *Experiencing God* and how impactful that book was on my faith. As I dug into *A Faith That Will Not Fail*, I felt the same hope. This book is bound to become a classic to help believers build upon spiritual disciples that will ground and ignite their faith.

—SUZANNE ELLER, bestselling author; Bible teacher; host, *Prayer Starters* podcast; cohost, *More Than Small Talk* podcast

Wow. What a wonderful book. If you need help navigating the senseless, the painful, the altogether terrible things that often come with living in a fallen world, this book is for you. I found myself in tears one moment, yet smiling the next. For in and through it all, Michele shows us how to find the God who is with us and working on our behalf, helping us build a faith that will not fail.

—JOANNA WEAVER, bestselling author, *Having a Mary Heart in a Martha World* and *Embracing Trust: The Art of Letting Go and Holding On to a Forever-Faithful God*

Full disclosure: Michele and I are friends, and I have seen her live out a lot of what she shares in her new devotional, *A Faith That Will Not Fail*. The reason I mention that is because in this book, she shares what has actually worked for her. This is not theory. This is not hopeful, untested promises. These are the actions that Michele has taken, the prayers she's prayed, the changes in thinking that she has experienced. Her life is proof that what is contained in this book has helped her recover, restore, and heal, and she is now sharing it with all of us. What a gift.

—KATHI LIPP, bestselling author; founder, The Red House Writers

For years, I've admired three-time cancer-survivor Michele Cushatt from afar, and in recent years as a precious friend. She is a woman of wisdom armed with grace, grit, and humility in the face of her life's relentless challenges. If you are weary but long to hold on to your faith, Michele has written this book for you. In *A Faith That Will Not Fail*, Michele shares a rich framework of Scripture, personal stories, and transforming spiritual practices that will inspire you to take one more step toward God in whatever you are facing today.

—BARB ROOSE, speaker; author, *Surrendered: Letting Go and Living Like Jesus*; *Joshua: Winning the Worry Battle*, and many more

This book is for anyone who has a weary heart and a tired faith. *A Faith That Will Not Fail* shows us how to build solid foundations for our spiritual lives so that we can weather the storms of life. Michele Cushatt guides us gently down a path to greater hope, faith, and resilience in the midst of all of life's troubles.

—MICHELLE AMI REYES, award-winning author, *Becoming All Things*; course founder, Seasoned with Grace

Michele shows up with yet another treasure trove of life-changing truth and life-giving practices. As a devoted reader and personal fan of Michele's, I soaked in this book with many "ah" and "yes" moments, especially in the areas of forgiveness and reconciliation. This book is a necessary and profound tool in a believer's toolbox of self-awareness and healing.

—KASEY VAN NORMAN, licensed professional counselor; bestselling author

A FAITH THAT WILL NOT FAIL

10 PRACTICES
to BUILD UP YOUR FAITH
WHEN YOUR WORLD
IS FALLING APART

MICHELE CUSHATT

ZONDERVAN
BOOKS

Library of Congress Cataloging-in-Publication Data

Names: Cushatt, Michele, 1971- author.
Title: A faith that will not fail : ten practices to build up your faith when your world is falling apart / Michele Cushatt.
Description: Grand Rapids : Zondervan, 2023. | Summary: "In A Faith that Will Not Fail, beloved author and Bible teacher Michele Cushatt presents ten practices that will strengthen your confidence in God's daily presence and power and help you discover a faith strong enough to endure even the most difficult circumstances"— Provided by publisher.
Identifiers: LCCN 2022050113 (print) | LCCN 2022050114 (ebook) | ISBN 9780310353034 (trade paperback) | ISBN 9780310353041 (ebook)
Subjects: LCSH: Faith. | Trust in God—Christianity. | Christian life. | BISAC: RELIGION / Christian Living / Devotional | RELIGION / Christian Living / Death, Grief, Bereavement
Classification: LCC BV4637 .C87 2023 (print) | LCC BV4637 (ebook) | DDC 234/.23—dc23/eng/20221228
LC record available at https://lccn.loc.gov/2022050113
LC ebook record available at https://lccn.loc.gov/2022050114

To those who suffer and yet long to believe:
Jesus' prayers are for you too.

Be alert and of sober mind. Your enemy the devil prowls around like a roaring lion looking for someone to devour. Resist him, standing firm in the faith, because you know that the family of believers throughout the world is undergoing the same kind of sufferings.

And the God of all grace, who called you to his eternal glory in Christ, after you have suffered a little while, will himself restore you and make you strong, firm and steadfast. To him be the power for ever and ever. Amen.

With the help of Silas, whom I regard as a faithful brother, I have written to you briefly, encouraging you and testifying that this is the true grace of God. Stand fast in it.

—I PETER 5:8–12

CONTENTS

4. THE PRACTICE OF RELINQUISHMENT

5. THE PRACTICE OF CONTENTMENT

6. THE PRACTICE OF SHALOM

7. THE PRACTICE OF FORGIVENESS

8. THE PRACTICE OF PERSPECTIVE

9. THE PRACTICE OF CONNECTION

10. THE PRACTICE OF WAITING

ACKNOWLEDGMENTS

The longer I live this side of heaven, the more aware I become of our inescapable interdependence. None of us arrives at this X on the timeline of life without the collective influence—big and small, visible and invisible—of the many individuals who have crossed our paths and left a mark there. My pilgrimage as a woman, faith struggler, and writer is no exception.

I won't attempt to list every name, because it would fill too many pages and I would no doubt still miss a few. But for this book, I'd like to mention those who have sharpened my faith, those rare few who have allowed me the space and grace to ask hard questions, to give voice to my doubts and big emotions, to wrestle with what I know and what I don't know (more the latter than the former), and who celebrate along with me that we've somehow stumbled our way to a faith that is a bit stronger and more refined than it once was. Hallelujah. These wise men and women, some still living and others even more alive through death, are part of my "cloud of witnesses." And this book and my faith are better for it.

Yvette. Juli. Bev. Vickie. Shantell. Angela. Tiffany. Carolyn. Brian. Andrew. Tangie. Danette. Adele. Patsy. Kathi. Susy. Cheri. Julie. Rhonda. Brianne. Bethany. Susan. Kate. Mom. Dad.

And to Jesus, the one who prayed for my faith before I knew I needed it and who called me to follow Him even knowing I would certainly fall: Your grace still takes my breath away. This is all for you. All the way home.

A RUN-DOWN FAITH

Therefore everyone who hears these words of mine and puts them into practice is like a wise man who built his house on the rock. The rain came down, the streams rose, and the winds blew and beat against that house; yet it did not fall, because it had its foundation on the rock.

—MATTHEW 7:24–25

The house didn't look like much the first time we saw it. Vacant for more than a year, neglected for a decade before that, the eight-acre property looked as if it was about to be swallowed up by nature. Various trees and bushes—some long dead, others barely alive—crowded the driveway and obscured the front walk. Noxious weeds covered what I assumed had once been a lush green lawn, their prickly edges scraping my feet as I walked the lot in my flip-flops. Gambel oak grew untamed, their skeletal arms reaching for the home's exterior walls.

I took it all in, comparing it with our manicured lawn back at home. What a mess.

Leaving the overrun outside behind, we followed the seller's realtor through the front door for a brief walk-through. It didn't take long to recognize similar signs of neglect. In addition to the lack of updates since its build twenty years before, everything from the bathrooms to the windows needed repairs. Days later, after a professional home inspection, we learned the house needed far more than cosmetic help.

It needed a gutting and rebuilding.

A new roof. New stucco and a full exterior paint job. An overhaul of the septic system. Repair of water damage to the hardwood floors. Multiple broken windows, a furnace on its last legs, and a dead air-conditioning unit that needed to be replaced by two new ones.

Those were the big items. The home had endured decades of daily life and Colorado's extreme weather. Without consistent attention, the wear and tear showed. To make it last, the next owner would need to invest significant time, sweat, and money, none of which we had in abundance. Troy and I both had demanding careers. And three of our six children still lived at home, early teenagers with a hard history and resulting needs. We already felt buried by daily life, without a move and renovation.

And yet, earlier that same year, a global pandemic caught the United States by surprise. In early March 2020, COVID-19 sent us home with the rest of the nation to quarantine for what we thought would be a couple of weeks. After months passed with no end in sight, we grew weary of our own walls. Isolation and virtual school frayed nerves and whittled away patience, the adults' as much as the children's. And the community we'd lived in for so long had grown congested, homes built one on top of the other. With church, work, and school relegated to the online space, we were no longer confined to a geographical locale. Moving suddenly felt like a viable option.

Then one day we stumbled on a home thirty minutes away sitting on eight wide-open acres, covered with scrub oak and evergreens, and with a view of the Rocky Mountains. Yes, the house was battered and worn. But so were we. Maybe that's why it felt like home.

"It has a good foundation," my contractor-husband said. "That's what I like about it. We can take care of everything else."

That's all I needed to hear.

Weeks later, we packed up and moved. During a pandemic. While working full time and helping three teens who were neck deep in online school. Who in their right mind decides to do a total home renovation in the middle of a global crisis?

We did. And I make no promises about the status of our minds. Trust me when I say I questioned our decision more than once.

Even so, my husband was right. The foundation proved solid. By the time we'd weathered the worst of the gutting, we ended up with a home turned haven right in the eye of a storm.

It was nineteenth-century German philosopher Friedrich Nietzsche who originally claimed, "That which doesn't kill us makes us stronger." The maxim, however callous when offered to a person in crisis, is true in part. Ease and comfort don't produce results. Resistance does. Like training for a marathon or lifting weights, it is our determination to push through difficulty that builds up our strength. Even so, we all know someone whose life disintegrated as a result of their challenges—Nietzsche's life included.

So why do storms devastate some homes while having little impact on others? Why does one person collapse in their crises while another appears stronger in spite of them? And why is it that some sufferers experience a deepening of faith while others end up denouncing it?

The disciples knew firsthand what it feels like to be caught in an unexpected storm. Luke tells the story:

> One day Jesus said to his disciples, "Let us go over to the other side of the lake."
>
> So they got into a boat and set out. As they sailed, he fell asleep. A squall came down on the lake, so that the boat was being swamped, and they were in great danger.

The disciples went and woke him, saying, "Master, Master, we're going to drown!"

He got up and rebuked the wind and the raging waters; the storm subsided, and all was calm. "Where is your faith?" he asked his disciples.

—LUKE 8:22–25

Mark calls the storm a "furious squall," a violent and sudden storm that overwhelmed the boat and terrified the disciples (Mark 4:37). They couldn't crank up the boat's V-8 engine or send up a flare for the Coast Guard. It was man versus nature, and nature proved stronger.

But the disciples missed one life-saving reality: Jesus was in their boat.

In the days before, the disciples witnessed Jesus perform breathtaking miracles, miracles that left no doubt as to His divine nature: a centurion's servant healed from a distance with a word from Jesus (Luke 7:1–10); a widow's only son raised from death back to life (vv. 11–16). This same miracle-working, death-defying Jesus sat only a few feet away from them in the boat.

As is often the case, the strength of the storm revealed the status of their faith.

"Don't you care if we drown?" they cried (Mark 4:38).

The truth of Jesus' identity and affection hadn't yet trumped the intensity of their circumstances. So when the storm and their fear raged, their faith in the Lord of the Storm flagged.

Over the past several years, we have found ourselves in the middle of furious global storms. Power-hungry rulers are killing innocents in the name of their personal appetites and evil agendas. Racial tensions that have long bubbled under the surface have come to an explosive head. Institutions that once seemed unshakeable are now mired in disrepute and doubt. Leaders who once appeared unflappable and untouchable have fallen ignobly off their platforms. Our confidence in the future and each other has waned to the point we no longer believe "the best is yet to come." And for many of us, the bedrock on which we stand shifts beneath our feet.

What do we do when the ground grows soft? Where do we turn to find a better footing?

Where is your faith?

Much like a house needs a solid foundation, the spiritual life must be grounded in the cement of faith. Church attendance, pithy spiritual quotes, and a playlist filled with Christian music aren't enough. Like home decor, they decorate the life of faith but don't ground it.

If our Christian activity isn't sourced in something substantial, it won't weather the worst of life's storms. The first time a squall rolls in, our rote religiosity will help about as much as wallpaper in a tornado. The well-decorated walls of the Christian life will disintegrate into rubble.

I know. Because this is what happened to me.

I was only a few months old when a man named Dave Mostek invited my dad to go to church with him and his wife. Dave and my dad worked together at State Farm Insurance in Southern California, two young men with young families—one a man of faith, the other a man fresh out of an abusive childhood and war in Vietnam. With a simple invitation, my dad discovered the hope of the gospel. As a result, the course of my life changed.

Whereas my dad lived twenty-seven years without faith, I don't remember a single day without its guiding force.[1] My earliest memories include images of Sunday church services, flannel-board Bible lessons, hymnals and four-part harmony, and potlucks filled with friends and nine-by-thirteen Pyrex pans of macaroni and cheese. I don't remember ever not believing in Jesus. Mine is a rich history filled with both faith practices and community, all of which gave me a solid basis of belief that serves me well to this day.

Even so, a soul needs more than rule-following religiosity to withstand the crucible of human experience. For the last thirty years, my life has been riddled by a series of significant storms: Divorce and single motherhood. Remarriage, stepfamily, and parenting challenges. Church conflict and division. Foster care and adoption of three children with a history of trauma. Loved ones with serious mental illness and health challenges. My dad's diagnosis of pancreatic cancer and his subsequent death. And then a cancer diagnosis of my own: squamous cell carcinoma of the tongue. Not once but three times.

It was the third diagnosis and subsequent extensive treatment that nearly did me in. By the end of those months of unfathomable suffering, only grace kept me alive.

It has now been seven years, and the miracle that is my life continues. For now. But daily I live with the repercussions of so much loss and trauma, as well as chronic pain and permanent disability, ever-present reminders of how close I came to the grave.

I'm often asked, "How do you still believe, after so many reasons not to?"

That's a good question.

But first, a story.

Before his death, Jesus dined with His disciples. It was Passover, the annual feast to remember Yahweh's deliverance of the Israelites from Egypt after hundreds of years of slavery. (See Exodus 11 and 12.) To those seated at the table, it was simply another Jewish celebration. Jesus knew otherwise.

This would be the Passover to which all the other Passovers had pointed. He would be the lamb sacrificed, His blood providing cover and allowing the sentence of death to pass over God's people, setting us free from our slavery to sin.

I've tried to imagine what that night must've been like for Jesus, agonizing over His upcoming suffering while also preparing the disciples for theirs. For three years, He'd poured into them, teaching and mentoring them. And yet they still didn't grasp what was about to take place. They didn't understand that their hopes were about to be hung on a cross. Instead, like teenagers vying for popularity, they argued about who was the greatest (Luke 22:24).

Which is why, I believe, Jesus turned to Simon Peter, a leader among them, with a few pointed words:

> "Simon, Simon, Satan has asked to sift all of you as wheat. But I have prayed for you, Simon, that your faith may not fail. . . ."
>
> But he replied, "Lord, I am ready to go with you to prison and to death."
>
> Jesus answered, "I tell you, Peter, before the rooster crows today, you will deny three times that you know me."
>
> —LUKE 22:31–34

For much of the last several years I've thought about this scene. Later that night, Peter faced his own crucible. Passionate but overly confident, he thought he was ready for the worst. He couldn't have been more wrong.

Jesus could see what Peter couldn't. Peter's good intentions would fail him long before he fled that night's garden. Which is why what happened next is so important.

Hidden in Jesus' poignant words to a perplexed Peter sit two extraordinary gifts.

First, a warning. "Satan has asked to sift all of you as wheat."

Oof. Talk about bad news. It's not every day you hear the devil is about to eat you for lunch.

And second, a promise. "I have prayed for you, Simon."

Whoa. Let that sink in. Jesus, the one Peter had declared to be "the Messiah, the Son of the living God" (Matt. 16:16), prayed for the man who would, before the end of the night, deny he ever knew Him. Long before the shock of Jesus' arrest shattered Peter's confidence, long before he tucked tail and fled in fear, long before he sat around a community fire and told accusing onlookers, "I don't know the man!" (Matt. 26:74), yes, long before Peter failed, Jesus prayed.

Peter's spiritual sifting wasn't a war that would be won by confidence or even the wielding of a sword. Instead, Peter needed the fortifying prayers of the Savior.

A warning (bad news). And a promise (ridiculously good news).

Jesus had all of His Father's power and authority at His fingertips. He could've called down fire and lightning or weapon-wielding angels, or even wrapped Peter in bubble wrap. Of all the things Jesus could've done to mitigate Peter's pain, He prayed.

He didn't pray for Peter's health, his family, his finances, or even his ability to fight back and escape arrest and death.

Instead, Jesus prayed for his faith.

In our places of suffering, we believe what is most at stake are our relationships, family, safety, financial security, health, or even our very lives. We think the diagnosis, divorce, or death is the worst that could happen.

We couldn't be more wrong.

Storms are a universal part of the human experience. No one escapes suffering or the day-to-day wear and tear on our human existence. "He causes his sun to rise on the evil and the good, and sends rain on the righteous and the unrighteous," Jesus reminds us (Matt. 5:45). And "in this world you will have trouble," He warns (John 16:33). Although our choices impact our path, we can't control the weather as we walk it. And just as weather reveals the stability of a home, suffering exposes the status of a person's faith.

8

Yes, I'm often asked how I can still believe after all I've endured. How did I survive so much suffering with my faith still intact? Here is my two-part answer.

First, like Peter, I take no credit for the faith that still grounds and guides me. As John Newton wrote in the lyrics of his now-famous hymn, "Amazing Grace":

> Through many dangers, toils and snares
> I have already come:
> 'tis grace has brought me safe thus far,
> and grace will lead me home.[2]

And second, although the grace of my Father carries me still, my years of following Jesus provided a foundation that helped me weather the worst life had to offer. As Bible teacher Jen Wilken says, "Spiritual disciplines nurture steadfastness. What we repeat in times of ease we will recall in times of hardship."[3] Like Peter, I've long been a disciple, albeit a poor one. I'm well intentioned but weak, at times overconfident and impulsive, and often underprepared. Although I love Jesus, I often fail Him. Even so, following Jesus has taught me practices that proved firm. Like a slow and steady renovation, these practices strengthened me a little at a time so that, when the storms came, my faith remained.

You may not have the same history with Jesus that I do. Some of you have journeyed much longer than I have, and others of you are just starting out. For those with an impressive Christian resume, don't mistake a devout life for a devoted love. It is possible to check all of the religion boxes and still miss out on real faith. The first is about performance; the second is about relationship.

And to those new to this Jesus thing, don't equate your lack of spiritual experience as weakness or, worse, a lesser love. Jesus said, "Truly I tell you, unless you change and become like little children, you will never enter the kingdom of heaven" (Matt. 18:3). Although your faith is new, you are uniquely able to approach Him without the arrogance that often accompanies religious performance. Come as you are. He's already head over heels for you.

GETTING THE MOST OUT OF THIS BOOK

My hope for this book is that it will be as practical as it is inspirational. Here are a few insights to help accomplish that aim.

First, *A Faith That Will Not Fail* covers ten faith practices, with five chapters per practice. This allows you the flexibility to read at your own pace or to read one practice per week (or month) in a small group, book club, or Bible study. I selected these particular practices, although they are perhaps unconventional, because they proved helpful to me and have biblical precedent.

However, this list of ten is not absolute or exhaustive. For example, Bible reading and memorization give me deep comfort and security when life is challenging. For that reason, you'll see abundant mention of Scripture throughout these pages. However, they're not one of the ten practices. The same is true for prayer. Initially, prayer sat at the top of the list. But the more I considered prayer in light of the other practices, the more I recognized its thread throughout each. Although it's missing from the list, prayer remains a critical part of a faith that will not fail.

Second, although it's tempting to follow these practices in a ten-step, linear process, life rarely falls into a tidy timeline. If you're reading in a group, practicality may require you to follow a calendar. But remember: the journey of faith seldom follows predictable steps. For example, practicing lament often occurs simultaneously with worship. Relinquishment isn't a one-and-done exercise but is ongoing. If you need a particular practice, allow yourself the freedom to skip chapters or sections, or to return to one that needs another look.

Finally, a word of warning: faith that endures can't be willed through hardworking, sleeve-rolling, boot-strapping determination. During the many faith-testing seasons of my fifty years of living, I have known Jesus for the vast majority of them. And from the age of seven, when I walked down the short aisle of my childhood church in central Illinois, I have sought to follow Him with heart, soul, mind, and strength. Ironically, the hardest seasons were also ones during which I was most disciplined: reading the Bible, going to church, and following some of the practices outlined in this book. No amount of effort prevented my pain. Spiritual practices hold no promise of escape. Suffering will come, and with it the questions. There will be days when you feel unmoored, even while doing your very best to hold on.

"If you do not stand firm in your faith, you will not stand at all," the Old Testament prophet Isaiah forewarns (Isa. 7:9).[4]

"So, if you think you are standing firm, be careful that you don't fall!" the New Testament apostle Paul challenges (1 Cor. 10:12).[5]

Indeed.

So what hope is there for us, we well-intentioned disciples who sometimes change our spiritual whims in moments of crisis and questions? We who fear our circumstances more than our Christ? How do we live as men and women of indefatigable faith when the world falls apart?

In his bestselling book *The Reason for God*, Timothy Keller, author and founding pastor of Redeemer Presbyterian Church in Manhattan, shares this illustration that helps to answer that question: "Imagine you are on a high cliff and you lose your footing and begin to fall. Just beside you as you fall is a branch sticking out of the very edge of the cliff. It is your only hope and it is more than strong enough to support your weight. How can it save you? If your mind is filled with intellectual certainty that the branch can support you, but you don't actually reach out and grab it, you are lost. If your mind is instead filled with doubts and uncertainty that the branch can hold you, but you reach out and grab it anyway, you will be saved. Why? It is not the strength of your faith but the object of your faith that actually saves you."

So how much faith in the branch does it take to be saved?

Just enough to reach for it.[6]

"Truly I tell you," Jesus said, "if you have faith as small as a mustard seed, you can say to this mountain, 'Move from here to there,' and it will move. Nothing will be impossible for you" (Matt. 17:20).

Peter knew far more about fish than faith. His office walls weren't papered with impressive seminary degrees and his socials didn't boast inspiring Christian dance videos. Jesus found Peter up to his ankles in mud and sand and called him to take hold of what He was offering: "Follow me."

A branch. *The Branch.*

Peter had just enough faith to reach for it. And when his world fell apart and his life was cut short, the Branch held, all the way home.

Jesus wants the same for you too, friend. He sees your fears and knows your questions.

Follow me, he says, hand extended.

You need only to reach for Him.

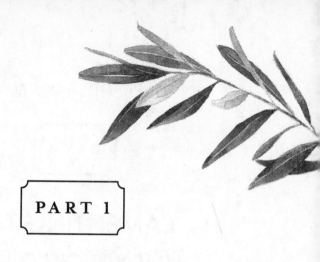

PART 1

THE PRACTICE OF LAMENT

The practice of lament may feel like an inauspicious place to begin. Often, in our desire to be faithful, we feel we must bury our big emotions. We think that to mourn our losses is to be less than faithful. So we tamp down grief, plaster on a spiritual smile, and pretend everything is okay. But we mustn't forget: before Jesus walked out of a tomb, He grieved in a garden. The tears we shed today only water the joy when all is healed. But first, we must acknowledge that things are not as they should be. Relationships break, loved ones die, bodies fail. These losses are worth our lament. When we give voice to the things that break our hearts, we add our tears to those of our Savior. Lament becomes a necessary part of the foundation of our faith, a faith that sees clearly the brokenness of the world and yet still believes in God's power to heal it.

$$\boxed{\text{DAY 1}}$$

LAMENTING THE UNEXPECTED LIFE

It is no part of the Christian vocation, then, to be able to explain what's happening and why. In fact, it is part of the Christian vocation not to be able to explain— and to lament instead. As the Spirit laments within us, so we become, even in our self-isolation, small shrines where the presence and healing love of God can dwell.
—N. T. WRIGHT, "CHRISTIANITY OFFERS
NO ANSWERS ABOUT THE CORONAVIRUS"

On Thursday, December 30, 2021, as another difficult year marked by a global pandemic ended, a wicked storm moved through Colorado. Although the storm came with neither rain nor snow, it delivered wind gusts at upwards of 80, 90, and 100 miles per hour. Sitting in our country home forty-five minutes south of Denver, I listened with concern to the howling wind rattling my windows. The months of September, October, and November had been unusually warm and dry, as if summer refused to concede to winter. Even December came with sunshine and very little snow. By December 30, we'd had nominal moisture and precipitation. I couldn't remember another December like it, where sweaters sat untouched in the closet and T-shirts filled the laundry.

After more than two decades in Colorado, I knew that windy days like this one—especially during hot and dry seasons—could spark devastating wildfires. Scrub oak cover most of our eight acres, easy kindling for a wayward spark or strike of lightning. They'd already shed their leaves in preparation for a winter that hadn't yet come. That Thursday, I listened to the wind as it whistled through our eaves, and I prayed for protection.

It was only an hour or two later that my biggest fear became a reality. Not for us or our neighbors but for the communities of Superior and Louisville, both sitting an hour north of us outside the city of Boulder.

Video footage soon surfaced showing shoppers running to their parked cars at a local Costco and residents fleeing their homes as the wind whipped smoke, ash, and sparks in every direction. The scene showed terror and chaos, an ordinary afternoon in a sluggish holiday week turned to tragedy. Later, I read news accounts of firefighters struggling to save structures at the risk of their own lives, fighting an unrelenting wind that outpaced them at every turn. In spite of their tireless effort, they realized minimal results. Within a single day, 1,084 homes were destroyed by the Marshall Fire. It took months to complete the investigation. No matter, the damage was done, the losses devastating.

I've struggled to wrap my mind around the magnitude of the destruction. In a single day, 1,084 homes, representing 1,084 families, were gone. So many memories, family heirlooms, and photos burned up in the span of minutes. Christmas presents opened only five days before turned to ash. Plans for a hopeful 2022 up in smoke.

Over the next months, these individuals and families filed insurance claims. Some were determined to rebuild, while others couldn't bear to return and decided to start fresh elsewhere. Regardless, life would continue. It always does. These now homeless families would build new homes, buy new furniture and appliances, make new memories and celebrate holidays in houses smelling of fresh paint and possibility.

But rebuilding takes years. And before these families could build the future, they had to attend to the ash of the past. Charred remains needed to be waded through to look for surviving treasures. Collapsed homes, little more than cinders, needed to be bulldozed. Losses needed to be cataloged, then submitted and explained to insurance companies. That alone could take months or years. Then, new plans needed to be drawn up, new permits pulled, construction crews hired, foundations laid. Taking stock of losses is a long, painful process.

This story and the painful recounting of it is the best representation I can think of for the biblical practice of lament. In Hebrew, lament means to wail, denoting a demonstrative form of grief, not merely an inward feeling of sorrow. In the Bible, lament is a critical part of worship. And it is always honest and expressive.

I realize that beginning a book about faith with the practice of lament might feel a bit intimidating. Wouldn't it make more sense to start with worship or gratitude? They certainly sound more hopeful. And yet as I considered my experience and likely that of the Marshall Fire survivors, I realized an important truth: hope without lament is like trying to build a home without dealing with the rubble.

To build an enduring faith, you and I must deal with the debris, cataloging the losses. I've learned that the grieving is the necessary first step to new living. Like clearing out the ash, lament allows the Spirit to help the heart heal and rebuild.

Just as the cross is necessary to the resurrection, lament is often the path to authentic worship. This means that if you are the one grieving, it is okay to weep. Your losses are worthy of lament. This isn't the way it's supposed to be, and it's okay to give voice to your anger and anguish.

And if you aren't the one grieving today, give thanks. And then make space for those who are. Add your tears to theirs. In that way, we together worship the only one who can heal.

Five-Minute Faith Builder

How long must I wrestle with my thoughts
and day after day have sorrow in my heart?
How long will my enemy triumph over me?

Look on me and answer, LORD my God.
Give light to my eyes, or I will sleep in death.

—PSALM 13:2–3

Pastor and author Dr. Glenn Packiam claims that true lament holds at least five purposes:

1. It is a form of praise.
2. It is proof of the relationship.
3. It is a pathway to intimacy with God.
4. It is a prayer for God to act.
5. It is a participation in the suffering of others.[7]

In my experience, lament is often a combination of most if not all of these, accompanied by the music of my individual grief. Consider these five purposes. Which do you need most right now? How might adding the practice of lament to your spiritual journey build up your faith? Record your thoughts in the margin or in a journal. Then pray this prayer:

Father, lament feels foreign and sometimes overwhelming. And yet Jesus cried out to you without fear. Teach me how to bring my grief to you, just as Jesus did, so that I can experience your touch of intimacy, healing, and peace.

DAY 2

THE PURPOSE OF LAMENT

The reason we don't want to feel is that feeling exposes
the tragedy of our world and the darkness of our hearts.
No wonder we don't want to feel. Feelings expose
the illusion that life is safe, good, and predictable.
—DR. DAN B. ALLENDER AND DR. TREMPER
LONGMAN III, *CRY OF THE SOUL*

Only two months after fighting for my life, I drove to a speaking engagement. The day before, I was too sick to get out of bed, concerned I might need to cancel. But by the next morning, I mustered my notoriously stubborn will, put on dress slacks, a blouse, and makeup, and drove to make an audio and video recording for an international radio program. Determined to press forward as if nothing had happened, I swallowed all the fear, pain, and loss and put on my best faith-filled smile, complete with gloss. This is what faithful Jesus-followers do, right? They keep pushing through, no matter the cost.

I still have a picture of that day in my phone. My clothes hung off my frame, black shadows circled my eyes, radiation burns still flared red on my neck. I looked like an ad for the walking dead. I still have no idea how—or why—I did such a thing. I wasn't being faithful. I was being foolish. Although my determination and stubbornness have served me well at times, in this case they were nothing but denial.

Although I fulfilled my speaking engagement, my grief would not be ignored. In the months that followed, the weight of cumulative loss soon bubbled to the surface and demanded a reckoning. For close to two years, I walked through a deep and dark abyss of lament. Some days it looked like weeping. Other days it looked like anger. Often, I feared I was going off the deep end. But soon I came to learn that my brain and body were doing what they were made to do: processing trauma and loss. I needed to stop trying to stiff-upper-lip my way through (which made it far worse) and instead allow myself to tell the truth about my pain.

I needed to practice lament.

To lament is "to express sorrow, mourning, or regret for often demonstratively . . . to regret strongly."[8] To lament is to give expression to the sorrow in your soul. In a sense, it is to make a formal complaint, but to take that complaint to the only one who has the power and authority to do anything about it: God Himself.

For a long time, I avoided lament. Reading Paul's instructions in Philippians 4:4–6 and 1 Thessalonians 5:16–18, I thought the Christian life meant perpetual positivity. It's true that we who believe in our one-day resurrection have good reason for joy. But the Bible also talks about the practice and worth of lament.

In Genesis 50:10, Joseph and his brothers practiced lament "loudly and bitterly" at the death of their father, Jacob.

Exodus tells us "the Israelites groaned in their slavery and cried out, and their cry for help because of their slavery went up to God. . . . So God looked on the Israelites and was concerned about them" (Ex. 2:23, 25).

In 2 Samuel, when David learns of the death of Saul and his son Jonathan, he pours out a lament (1:17–27).

Psalm 102 is titled "A prayer of an afflicted person who has grown weak and pours out a lament before the LORD." Many additional psalms are lamentations, not praise. (See Psalms 6, 10, 13, 22, 38, 42, 43, and 130, among others.)

The book of Jeremiah, "the weeping prophet," is a book of complaints. It is also the longest book in the Bible, containing more words than any other book.[9]

And I can't fail to mention the book of Lamentations, which is exactly what its name implies: a book of lament.

This is a small sample of lament throughout Scripture. And yet in our modern worship experience, the practice of lament is notably absent. I believe we're missing an essential building block of our faith.

What is the purpose of lament? N. T. Wright, author and senior research fellow at Wycliffe Hall in Oxford, England, wrote an article for *Time* in which he claims that "the point of lament, woven thus into the fabric of the biblical tradition, is not just that it's an outlet for our frustration, sorrow, loneliness and sheer inability to understand what is happening or why. The mystery of the biblical story is that God also laments. Some Christians like to think of God as above all that, knowing everything, in charge of everything, calm and unaffected by the troubles in his world. That's not the picture we get in the Bible."[10]

First, lament gives voice to both our grief and our guilt. Like any open wound, neglect and disregard put you at greater risk for infection and scarring, even death. When we don't give it voice, grief festers, ultimately consuming us with misery. But when we acknowledge our sorrow in the presence of the Savior, healing begins.

And second, the practice of lament not only allows us to identify and name our grief but also directs us to the source of our hope. Our grief and guilt can find redemption only when we turn to the one who holds the power and authority to redeem. As author Michelle Reyes says, "Let your lament be your declaration of hope in God in the midst of hard things."[11]

To complain to anyone else may bring temporary comfort, but they hold no power to heal. And often we end up deeper in despair. But to voice our complaints to God tells the truth about our circumstances and acknowledges who is able to deliver.

Dan Allender and Tremper Longman III, in their book *Cry of the Soul*, discuss at length the role emotions play in our growing knowledge of God. "A determination to resolve our emotional struggles inevitably subordinates God as a servant of our healing rather than a person to be praised. Rather than focusing on trying to change our emotions, we are wiser first to listen to them. They are a voice that can tell us how we are dealing with a fallen world, hurtful people, and a quizzical God who seldom seems to be or do what we expect of Him."[12]

"I wait for the LORD," the psalmist writes, "my whole being waits, and in his word I put my hope. . . . Israel, put your hope in the LORD, for with the LORD is unfailing love and with him is full redemption" (Ps. 130:5, 7). When we pour our tears out before the Lord, we will discover full redemption. Not partial. Not temporary. Full.

"It is finished," Jesus said as His body gave way to death (John 19:30). And with that, my lament, however deep, ultimately ends in redemption.

Yours does too.

Five-Minute Faith Builder

Blessed are those who mourn, for they will be comforted.
—Matthew 5:4

Author Philip Yancey writes, "In grief, love and pain converge."[13] What have you lost? Big or small, what are the people, plans, purposes that, somehow, have not turned out like you hoped? One exercise that helped me take a giant step toward healing was to give myself permission to name my losses. It sounds indulgent, even counterproductive. Simply, I sat on the patio in my back yard with a pen and an empty notebook and made a bulleted list of the things I mourned. And as I named my grief, God started to heal my heart. Will you consider doing the same? Take a few moments to start your list. The purpose isn't rumination but release. Name your losses. Go ahead, friend. He already knows.

THE PRACTICE OF LAMENT

DAY 3

LAMENTING OUR EARTHLY LOSSES

There was plenty of suffering for us to get through. Therefore, it was necessary to face up to the full amount of suffering, trying to keep moments of weakness and furtive tears to a minimum. But there was no need to be ashamed of tears, for tears bore witness that a man had the greatest of courage, the courage to suffer.

—VIKTOR E. FRANKL, *MAN'S SEARCH FOR MEANING*

Fifty-year-olds shouldn't want to run away.

Running away is for temperamental ten-year-olds with irrational threats and backpacks in hand: "I'm running away! All the other kids get to stay up late. It's not fair!"

Running away is for children, not grown adults.

Even so. I wanted to wail with all the world's mistreated ten-year-olds, "It's not fair!"

Life was too much. I felt like I was suffocating, the mounting responsibilities and impossibilities of each day slowly cutting off my air.

I couldn't take it anymore, all the long and hard days lined up one after the other without any end or relief in sight.

I gave the suitcase in my closet a glance. But I wasn't ten years old anymore. Instead, I grabbed my running shoes. Then, slipping the leash around the neck of Vesper, my black Lab and running partner, I headed outside and toward the street, shutting the back door with extra gusto. I couldn't run away, but I could run. And I felt mad enough to run for a million miles.

I didn't make it to the end of our block before the anger gave way to weeping. I stopped, gulping air in an attempt to calm down, hoping my neighbors were too busy with their perfect lives to notice the wreck of mine. With a shake of my head, I looked to the sky, my many losses flowing down my face.

It's not fair! It wasn't fair that I'd dreamed of ministry and married a pastor only to end up divorced and a single mom at the age of twenty-seven. It wasn't fair that my second marriage had come with so many painful and complicated remarriage and stepfamily dynamics. It wasn't fair that I'd survived cancer once in my thirties only to face it two more times in my forties, all while watching my father die of cancer when I needed him to help walk me through my own. Then there was the fostering and adopting of three more kids when we were finally about to be empty nesters for the first time. And on top of that, each day came with the lingering pain and disability of a postcancer body.

Enough, God. Isn't it enough?

The fury that propelled me in running shoes proved the anger merely a smokescreen for my grief. A lifetime of losses gutted me, and I felt buried by my inescapable circumstances. Yes, I knew I still had plenty to be grateful for. I had a home to live in, food to eat, a family to care for. And yet the life we lived wasn't easy. The reality of it crushed, compounded by the truth that it would likely never change. There was no promised land for me on this side of heaven. As with the Sons of

Korah in Psalm 42, my tears were my food day and night, and justifiably so.

This wasn't the first time I'd experienced a tidal wave of grief, and it would not be the last. I have many such days when the losses I carry feel like a too-heavy backpack that I cannot put down. They accompany me, reminding me of what is, what could've been, and what will never be. Well-intentioned acquaintances, unable to grasp my daily life, attempt to explain my suffering: "Look how God is using you!" and "God must have a big place for you in heaven!" Though their attempts to encourage are sincere, they offer no relief. Their words do little to lighten the weight. And so I continue, with jogging shoes and backpack, lugging around my losses and weeping at the end of my block.

I know my reality isn't much different from so many others'. The details of our stories may differ, but each of us carries grief. Regardless of its source, we feel a sense of unfairness. Children shouldn't be afraid of those who should be caring for them. Careers shouldn't end without warning, leaving the unemployed without the means to pay the bills. Nations shouldn't live in fear of revolution, churches in fear of division, marriages in fear of dissolution. And yet here we are. Governments crumple, churches divide, marriages dissolve, jobs disappear. And in the wake of such losses, humanity weeps: *It's not fair!*

Author N. T. Wright says it best: "Lament is what happens when people ask, 'Why?' and don't get an answer."[14]

Exactly.

It was lament that made me near desperate to run away, lament that came out in anger and tears while jogging to the end of my street. Buried lament leads to a bitter soul. But lament expressed to a loving God is a soul's vocalization of grief to the only one who can take pain's discordant notes and write them into a song.

Lamenting our earthly losses is not only healing, it is holy, as much a part of worship as is a heart full of joy.

Five-Minute Faith Builder

LORD, *you are the God who saves me;*
day and night I cry out to you.
May my prayer come before you;
turn your ear to my cry.

—PSALM 88:1–2

For many of us, the practice of lament does not come easily. Perhaps someone taught us that showing emotion is weak. Or maybe we fear that telling God the truth about how we feel is disrespectful. For me, I was afraid that if I gave voice to my grief, the dam would break and the emotions would take me under. Consider any reactions or resistance you feel toward the practice of lament and write them down in a journal or in the margin of this book. Get as clear as you can as to why you avoid the practice of lament. Then read Psalm 88, a prayer of lament. Highlight or underline anything you notice that could provide new freedom in this practice.

DAY 4

MOURNING OUR
SPIRITUAL LOSTNESS

For what am I to myself without You,
but a guide to my own downfall?
—AUGUSTINE OF HIPPO, *CONFESSIONS*

For months, I have watched along with the rest of the world as
Russia, led by President Vladimir Putin, has tirelessly and without provocation attacked the sovereign nation of Ukraine. It has been
unending, this onslaught, and my heart aches with every news update
on the war and the cost of human life. Even as I sit safely ensconced in
my home office, I know that people in Eastern Europe do not feel the
same comfort. The war sits at their front door. And when I dare to consider their predicament seriously, I must admit that advanced weaponry
means I'm not so distant or so safe either. All it would take is the whim
of a madman to deliver all of us back to dust.

I feel helpless to predict exactly how all of this will pan out.
Journalists and political scientists are doing their best to anticipate
Putin's next move, an attempt to preempt disaster. But no one knows. It

is a chess game with myriad potential outcomes. By the time this book makes it to print (assuming we are not dust), this high-stakes game will have progressed through thousands of moves and countermoves. Will the game be over? Or just begun?

There seems to be no end to humanity's capacity for injustice. This morning, the news told of a man who assaulted his girlfriend and mom, the discovery of a stolen box of human heads, a fire under investigation for arson, and refugees fleeing Eastern Europe in the hundreds of thousands, most with little more than what they can carry. Closer to home, I read my Twitter feed followed by a heated email from our home association detailing various disputes between homeowners. The vitriol in both places appalls me. Are we not friends and neighbors? And yet I cannot avoid looking within the walls of my own home. Only yesterday I almost lost my cool with a certain fourteen-year-old. After enduring hours of attitude, I nearly reciprocated in kind. I didn't, by some small miracle. But I struggled to share the same air with her for the remainder of the day. And my resistance to grace waged its own war.

Lord, have mercy. Is there no end to our depravity?

In Matthew 23, Jesus candidly addresses His contemporary religious leaders with a series of "woes." Without apology or any attempt to mute his language, Jesus calls out their unconscionable behavior, promising consequences for those who commit injustice in the name of religion. We see Jesus' righteous anger, the heat of his holy frustration against those who use their religious position for power and oppression.

Jesus' anger is justified. But anger alone isn't enough. Shortly after, Matthew notes a paradoxical shift in Jesus' countenance. He goes from condemnation to compassion, seemingly in the span of moments: "Jerusalem, Jerusalem, you who kill the prophets and stone those sent to you, how often I have longed to gather your children together, as a hen gathers her chicks under her wings, and you were not willing" (Matt. 23:37).

With a cry of the heart, Jesus expresses both outrage and ache over Israel's lostness. He condemns their continual rejection of everything good and holy while also expressing compassion for their need for rescue. In an extravagant show of tenderness, He uses the feminine imagery of a mother hen to convey the depth of both His desire for intimacy and His grief over the lack of it. Ligonier Ministries sums up this image of Jesus in this way: "Jesus' lament shows us that human suffering, considered in itself, does not please the Almighty. Although God has ordained Jerusalem's destruction, His revealed will in Scripture proves He has 'no pleasure in the death of the wicked' (Ezek. 33:11). . . . We are not perfectly holy and have no inherent right to execute wrath. How then can we take pleasure in the death of the sinner if God finds no pleasure in the death of the wicked? Our hearts should be broken, not gleeful, when we see someone destroy himself on account of his evil. As you lament the moral degeneracy of our culture, can others hear sadness in your voice?"[15]

When I read the news, scour social media, and reflect on my posture at home, I see far more evidence of outrage than grief. Although we may be skilled at calling out injustice, we are far less practiced in confessing it. When was the last time you mourned the world's lostness, including your own? As you talk about the headlines, can others hear the sadness in your voice? Our self-righteous goodness can be a cloak for arrogance. We in the church cause considerable harm when we climb up on the flimsy pedestals of our religion so we can look down on those who are less righteous. That posture couldn't be any less like Jesus (Phil. 2:5–8).

Without Jesus, each one of us is utterly and hopelessly lost. Let's lament our corporate sinfulness. Let's grieve our world's lostness. And thus add to Jesus' tears our own.

Five-Minute Faith Builder

How long, Lord, must I call for help,
but you do not listen?
Or cry out to you, "Violence!"
but you do not save?
Why do you make me look at injustice?
Why do you tolerate wrongdoing?
Destruction and violence are before me;
there is strife, and conflict abounds.

—HABAKKUK 1:1–3

The New Testament book of James is sometimes called the "blue jeans gospel." Its overall message is a practical one: how to live out our faith, especially in difficult circumstances. This context is critical when reading James 4:8–9: "Come near to God and he will come near to you. Wash your hands, you sinners, and purify your hearts, you double-minded. Grieve, mourn and wail. Change your laughter to mourning and your joy to gloom." Sobering words, yes? We don't enjoy anything that hinders our happiness. But James instructs us to include grief and mourning as part of our faith practice. Today, let's practice lament by allowing ourselves to grieve the state of our world. Take a moment to scan the headlines about your nation, city, and neighborhood if you haven't already. Then take what you read and the emotion it stirs to the same Jesus who cried over Jerusalem.

DAY 5

THE GIFT OF SHARED SUFFERING

The way to a stronger faith usually lies along the
rough path of sorrow. . . . What do I not owe to the
hammer and the anvil, the fire and the file?
—CHARLES SPURGEON

The text from my husband pinged my phone in the early hours of the workday.

"Dwight died last night."

Troy had been friends with Dwight for more than thirty years, and I've known him as long as I've known Troy. We did life and ministry with him. He was our age, healthy, strong. No risks or warning signs. Just an average, fifty-four-year-old male whom we loved.

A few weeks before, Dwight had come down with COVID. And for whatever reason, it hit him harder than most. Within a couple of weeks, he was hospitalized, and shortly after, he was gone.

Just like that.

This loss hit us hard. Life and death don't play by our rules. I know this. Even so I cried more than once over the days that followed, weeping for his four children and fiancee. I prayed for God to be extraordinarily present with them while I continued to ask Him questions to which I won't get answers this side of heaven.

And then I read these words I wrote nearly seven years ago in the pages of my second book, *I Am:* "God doesn't expect me to dance at His empty tomb without weeping at His cross. I don't have to hide my grief or pretend I'm stronger than I am."[16]

Sometimes God uses my own words to remind me of a truth He taught me long ago. Grief, as messy as it is, isn't a lack of faith. It's honest worship. When we grieve what has been lost and ask questions to which we receive no answers, we place ourselves squarely at the foot of an unjust cross. That means our screams of anguish are, in fact, worship. A raw and bared worship that throws itself at the only one able to make the world right again. But, at times, individual lament isn't enough. Isolation doesn't give our grief full expression. Instead, we need the comfort of collective grief, of mourning together. That is why, a couple of weeks later, those of us who knew and loved Dwight gathered for his memorial service, to lament together.

It's easy to share in the suffering of those who are close to us. But what about that of individuals, communities, and nations that are not our own?

In January 2022, an Asian American woman living in New York City, Michelle Go, prepared to board a subway. Within moments, she became the victim of a hate crime when a man pushed her off the platform into the path of an oncoming train. A handful of news articles told us the story with grim and sensational details, and many of us consumed them. But did we grieve? We didn't know Michelle Go. Why would her life and loss impact us? And yet how can we fully participate in this human existence without allowing another's pain to become our own?

In response to the story of Michelle Go, Michelle Ami Reyes, a friend and an author who speaks passionately about the importance of connecting across cultures, published an article offering three practical ways for churches to participate in corporate lament.

> The path for a church to become a space of racial healing is complex, but one element that every church should include is a regular rhythm of corporate lament. . . .
>
> Are your church leaders vocal from the pulpit every week about calling out communal sins (e.g., racism, sexism, misogyny, abuse, etc.)?
>
> Do you regularly practice lament on Sunday mornings in worship songs, sermons, and in pastoral and communal prayers?
>
> Do you host regular gatherings of prayer and lament (weekly, monthly, quarterly, etc.) as a church in which congregants are given space to share their pains and grieve and pray together as the body of Christ? . . .
>
> That's what churches need to do in the midst of tragedies, whether racial, natural, or otherwise. Stop what you're doing. Tend to your congregation. Rethink the liturgy, the sermon, the tone of your Sunday morning. Give special attention to the tragedy now ripping through your community. Speak to your people, acknowledge their pain, cry with them, look to Scripture, and point them to Christ.[17]

Corporate lament sits at the heart of the gospel. God Himself left the comfort of heaven to join the collective human experience through Jesus' life and death. He entered into our suffering so we, having been assured our lives matter to Him, can enter into suffering with each other.

This is our challenge. And this is our privilege.

Five-Minute Faith Builder

Rejoice with those who rejoice; mourn with those who mourn.

—ROMANS 12:15

Paul's instructions in Romans 12:15 follow on the heels of his urging readers to "offer your bodies as a living sacrifice, holy and pleasing to God" (v. 1). Mourning with those who mourn is part of our humble service as the body of Christ. This collective sharing in each other's suffering—corporate lament—can be practiced in a variety of environments: during a church service, while praying with a small group or Bible study group, or even with a close friend or with your children before bed. For example, our family often prays for the homeless population around Denver. We acknowledge their suffering, especially when extreme weather exacerbates it, and we ask God to deliver relief. Our corporate lament also includes our practical support of homeless ministries and agencies, financially and otherwise. But it begins with suffering alongside them in prayer. How can you share in another's suffering today? Pray this prayer:

Father, you see the suffering of those around me more clearly than I do. Open my eyes to see what I may have missed. Move my heart with what moves yours.

Then, after a moment or two of listening, write down whoever God brings to mind, and commit to action.

$$\boxed{\text{PART 2}}$$

THE PRACTICE
OF WORSHIP

For those who grew up in church, the word *worship* is so familiar that it might have lost some of its meaning. For those who are new to faith, the word may be as unfamiliar as a foreign language. *Worship* comes from a root that means "worth-ship," or to acknowledge the worthiness of someone or something. We worship plenty of subjects: movie stars, loved ones, ice cream. But when we're suffering, a lesser object of worship can't deliver. So the practice of worship—acknowledging the reality and worth of God—becomes essential to a faith that can weather the worst of circumstances. For when we take time to consider the magnitude and mystery of our God, the creator of the universe and the lover of our souls, our pain is reoriented in the context of His presence and power. And we discover, in spite of everything, we are not alone.

THE BEAUTY OF GOD

*If someone had seen our faces on the journey from
Auschwitz to a Bavarian camp as we beheld the
mountains of Salzburg with their summits glowing
in the sunset, through the little barred windows of
the prison carriage, he would never have believed
that those were the faces of men who had given up
all hope of life and liberty. Despite that factor—
or maybe because of it—we were carried away by
nature's beauty, which we had missed for so long.*
—VIKTOR E. FRANKL, *MAN'S SEARCH FOR MEANING*

Less than thirty minutes ago, I woke up and crawled out of bed to start my day. Tiptoeing as quietly as possible, which my husband claims is not all that quiet, I slipped into my robe and sneaked out of our bedroom with a slow close of the door.

This is my daily custom. I rise before the dawn, while the rest of my family sleeps. As our automatic espresso machine fills a single cup with creamy coffee, I grab a book or my Bible—sometimes both—and settle into my leather office chair or family-room couch, cocooned in my favorite blanket.

I don't recall the Bible passage I'd been reading that day nor exactly how much time passed before it happened. But I clearly remember how, in the middle of a sentence, the pages of my Bible morphed from onion-skin white to a soft shade of pink. Inhaling, I looked up to see the family room soaked in color. The once gray and navy throw pillows looked nearly purple. The walls—painted the year before a soft Sherwin-Williams Repose Gray—appeared orange. The cause, of course, was not that someone had repainted my walls or recovered my pillows. Rather, they reflected the vibrant pink rays of the rising sun streaming in through our windows. Leaving my blanket and Bible behind, I opened the back door, walked outside, and looked up.

The sky was awash in fire. I've seen my share of stunning sunrises during my tenure in Colorado. But I'd never witnessed such brilliance, such shocking glory. I grabbed my phone, determined to capture it with a few pictures. I wanted to preserve the moment like a child's handprint in wet cement.

Instead, each picture proved more disappointing than the last.

In no time at all, pink, orange, and purple hues faded, leaving ordinary gray-blue hues behind. Glory gave way to the ordinary. Caught up in capturing the beauty, I missed out on the adoration of it. I'd been distracted by the reflection rather than awed by the source. And by the time I realized my mistake, the moment was gone.

Beauty is a means through which I experience God's presence. I feel Him when I hike a mountain trail or sit at the edge of a tumbling stream or watch the sun fall below the horizon at the end of another day. I hear Him in the light dance of a piano concerto and see Him in a symphony conductor's blazing passion. Perhaps it is because beauty can't be explained or contained. There's a wildness, an untamed and unexplained way beauty moves a soul and inspires belief. The mystery of it compels me to marvel.

But to worship beauty itself is much like trying to capture a brilliant sunrise with an amateur camera. Even the best shot is only a marginal representation of the real thing. It's not the object of beauty itself. Rather, it's the camera's best reflection of it.

In his work *The Weight of Glory*, C. S. Lewis describes it this way: "At present we are on the outside of the world, the wrong side of the door. We discern the freshness and purity of morning, but they do not make us fresh and pure. We cannot mingle with the splendors we see. But all the leaves of the New Testament are rustling with the rumor that it will not always be so. Some day, God willing, we shall get *in*."[18]

Evidence of God's presence is everywhere. We hear it in the sound of birdsong as spring returns yet again after a hard winter. We feel it in the warm arms of a trusted friend's reassuring embrace. We see Him in the miracle of pregnancy and the breathtaking joy of a baby's birth. We recognize His presence in the sun's warmth and the brilliance of the stars dotting the night sky. We hear it in the harmony of a musician's composition and see it in the colors on an artist's canvas. The beauty around us speaks to the existence of the creator of it. And yet as much as we marvel and gasp, all of these evidences are single brushstrokes of a great masterpiece, unfinished notes of our ultimate hallelujah.

In Romans 1:20, Paul writes, "For since the creation of the world God's invisible qualities—his eternal power and divine nature—have been clearly seen, being understood from what has been made, so that people are without excuse." Each moment we take in creation, we get a glimpse of God's glory. But we mustn't worship beauty itself but rather the creator of it. And when we rightly worship the one who holds nature and music and art in His creative hands, we have the beginnings of faith.

Don't bother trying to contain Him in a picture. You will find the medium too small for Him. Instead, allow yourself to be overcome. The same God who paints the sky in glory calls you by name. And He's worth waking up early to worship.

Five-Minute Faith Builder

The heavens declare the glory of God;
  the skies proclaim the work of his hands.
Day after day they pour forth speech;
  night after night they reveal knowledge.
They have no speech, they use no words;
  no sound is heard from them.
Yet their voice goes out into all the earth,
  their words to the ends of the world.

—PSALM 19:1–4

What aspect of the creation speaks most to you of the Creator? Evidence of God's reality is abundant. Look for Him—in the vivid color of a fresh bouquet of flowers, the smell of a pine tree, the music of a loved one's laughter. When you find evidence of Him, write it down here or in a journal. Notice and acknowledge the worth of the one who created it all. "All creation declares . . ." Yes, it does. Now add your voice to creation's worship with this simple prayer:

God, today I see evidence of you in _____
and in _____. *How beautiful you are! Thank you for the fresh assurance that you are present and at work in all things. Strengthen my faith with this truth.*

$$\boxed{\text{DAY 2}}$$

THE TERROR OF GOD

*The practice of non-violence requires
a belief in divine vengeance.*
—MIROSLAV VOLF

When I told my friend what had happened, I could see anger tense the muscles of her neck. She's not one given to explosive anger. No throwing plates or punching walls. She's one of the most positive people I know, in control at all times. Even so, I needed her to be upset on my behalf. And this time she was.

A longtime relationship had broken trust in a painful way. As a result, I felt used and devalued, taken advantage of. I poured out the story, the injustice and rejection.

"Why does this keep happening to me?" I cried. "I gave everything I had, and in the end it didn't make any difference." Perspective would come a couple of days later, but in that moment, I felt only heartbreak.

My friend already knew that. She knew how hard I'd worked to honor the relationship, how much I had sacrificed. My loyalty was total and complete. Unfortunately, I'd discovered that loyalty wasn't reciprocated.

With tears running down my cheeks, I looked at my friend's face, recognizing the simmering beneath the surface. Most would not notice. But after years of friendship, I did.

"Are you angry?" I asked.

It took her only a second. "Yes, I am. What they did wasn't right. It's not okay for people to treat someone else that way."

And with those words, I exhaled. It's what I needed most in that moment. Her anger validated my wound. I needed to know that she saw the injustice and that her love for me stirred a response, if only in this private moment. Although the circumstances would not change, her righteous anger softened my own, muting any need to retaliate against the one who hurt me. It was enough to know that the injustice I felt was legitimate and that I was not alone in it.

We've all had moments like these, when we need someone to share our indignation. Rather than pat us on the head and tell us to cheer up, they sit down with us in our fury and offer to smash a plate right along with us. It's empathy, an entering and sharing in the struggle. And it brings more healing than we often realize.

Of course, it can go too far. Left unchecked, shared empathy over injustice can become toxic, and in extreme cases lead to mob violence. Pastor and author Scott Sauls describes this well: "You know that relationship and community have gone toxic when the bond of having a common enemy becomes stronger, and more compelling and delicious, than the bond of shared commitment to reconciliation and truth."[19] When we stoke the fires of each other's rage without restraint, it spreads like wildfire, consuming whatever is in its path, including ourselves. I suspect we've all known moments like this too. And it is anything but healing.

What we need is someone who embodies absolute justice *and* perfect love. God Himself.

I often hear people voice their struggle with the God of the Bible. "I can't believe in a God of wrath. I can't get behind a God who would send people to hell. God is supposed to be good. And if He's not, I don't want any part of Him." I get it. For the longest time I couldn't stomach the thought of God being angry. How could I pray to a God of wrath? How could I come to Him with all my failures and struggles and heartbreaks if He could strike me down on a whim?

It wasn't until I faced a series of hard injustices that I finally understood the kindness and righteousness of God's anger.

After spending my childhood praying for a Christian marriage, I ended up a rejected, divorced single mother by the time I was twenty-seven.

After dedicating my life to serving the church, I ended up abandoned and rejected by many churchgoing people who, although well intentioned, did not know how to embrace someone who was flawed and broken.

After building an entire ministry around teaching and speaking, I had cancer that robbed me of my voice and forever changed my ability to speak. Not once but three times.

But all of this pales in comparison with the pain I feel when I consider the wounds my father and my youngest children carry from the early years of their lives. And when I consider their unjust suffering and how it has become my own, I'm angry. Very angry.

In these moments, I need to know that our God has the capacity for anger. It is not enough for me that He is a God of love. I need to know that His love also spurs action, that somehow His deep agape for me and my children, for my friends and my family, and for so many others throughout the world who suffer far more unspeakable injustices than I do will cause Him to rise up and fight for us.

When I think about it this way, I don't want a soft God. I want a God whose goodness is so good that He cannot—will not—tolerate all that is wrong. I want a God of righteousness and wrath who is also the perfect expression of love.

A God of our own making is far too small. We need a God who is uncontainable, unfathomable. We need a God of love whose neck turns

THE TERROR OF GOD

red when He sees babies trafficked and genocides enacted. We need a God who, one day, will cease restraint and announce with a holy bellow that shakes our walls into dust: *Enough!*

This is who He is. Hallelujah, this is Who He Is. It should terrify us. But may it also comfort us.

Five-Minute Faith Builder

LORD, I have heard of your fame;
I stand in awe of your deeds, LORD.
Repeat them in our day,
  in our time make them known;
  in wrath remember mercy.

—HABAKKUK 3:2

In our desire to make God accessible, we sometimes make Him less powerful. But a weak God can't redeem all that is wrong with our world. We need a God who is simultaneously terrifying and loving, righteous and merciful, mighty and compassionate. Spend a few minutes considering God's ultimate authority and power as you read Isaiah 2 and Isaiah 6:1–8. Highlight any words that talk about the terror of God. Don't try to soften His holy edges. Instead, see Him for who He is in all His power and glory. Then consider how this holy, righteous, and just God is able to deliver the comfort and security you crave. He alone can heal what is broken. He alone can make right all the wrongs. He alone can deliver true justice where there has been none. Because He alone is both holy and loving.

$$\boxed{\text{DAY 3}}$$

THE NEARNESS OF GOD

*What makes life worthwhile is having a big
enough objective, something which catches our
imagination and lays hold of our allegiance,
and this the Christian has in a way that no other
person has. For what higher, more exalted, and more
compelling goal can there be than to know God?*
—J. I. PACKER, KNOWING GOD

If progressive napping is a thing, my dog, Vesper, is a master of it.

My home office sits at the back of our house, with a large seven-foot picture window giving a full and unobstructed view of the mountain behind us. It also faces southeast, which means that when the sun comes up in the morning, its rays pour through my office window and land squarely on my office rug.

That is where you'll find Vesper every single day between the hours of 8:00 a.m. and noon. Napping.

But it is progressive napping. In a fashion similar to the progressive dinners our church family hosted when I was a child—the ones where you progress from house to house for the different courses of a dinner, including appetizer, main dish, and dessert—my dog, bless her little heart, progresses across my office rug as she follows the course of the sun. First thing in the morning, as I'm starting another day of work, she finds the sun on my rug and stops, drops, and falls into a deep, snore-filled slumber, the sun's rays warming her shiny black belly. An hour later, when the sun has moved a foot or two across the rug, she wakes up, stretches with a very loud yawn, walks over to the new spot of sunshine, flops down with her belly square in the center of the beam, and falls right back to sleep.

This is her pattern, from the moment the sun rises until it moves beyond the reach of my window. Then she returns to her dog bed, dejected (if it's possible for a dog to be such a thing), and waits to start the routine all over again the following day.

Of course, progressive napping is a lot of work for a lazy old dog, all that getting up and flopping down, falling asleep only to wake up and fall back to sleep again. But she doesn't seem to mind. It's worth it to bask in the sun's presence. As I watch her, I think, *I wish I were a dog.*

When God called Moses and the Israelites to leave Egypt and travel across a desert wilderness to Canaan, the land He promised them, Moses' greatest fear wasn't lack of food and water and shelter. What Moses knew he needed most of all, every step of the way, was God's presence: "Then Moses said to him, 'If your Presence does not go with us, do not send us up from here. How will anyone know that you are pleased with me and with your people unless you go with us? What else will distinguish me and your people from all the other people on the face of the earth?'" (Ex. 33:15–16).

Moses knew they wouldn't survive the journey ahead on their own. So he asked for what they needed most. God's presence with them. Smart man.

"The Lord replied, 'My Presence will go with you, and I will give you rest.' . . . And the Lord said to Moses, 'I will do the very thing you have asked, because I am pleased with you and I know you by name'" (vv. 14, 17).

For the next forty years, God's presence went with Moses and the Israelites, every step through the wilderness and to the promised land, in the form of a pillar of cloud by day and a pillar of fire by night (Ex. 40:36–38). When the cloud moved, the people moved. When the cloud stopped, the people stopped. They took their cues from God's presence because they knew they were lost without Him.

Here's the real good news, for you and for me, thousands of years after those Israelites in the desert: the pillars of cloud and fire foreshadowed a greater presence, Emmanuel, God with Us. Knowing we'd never make it on our own, Jesus came to do life with us. And now, on the other side of His death and resurrection, God's Spirit lives in us. Morning or night, awake or asleep, sun shining or rain falling, He is right here. And just as the sun warms Vesper's belly and brings her peace and rest, He longs for you and me to settle into the warmth of the Son.

God is with you. Do you feel His Spirit within? Close your eyes and allow your heart to soak up His nearness. You are not alone.

Five-Minute Faith Builder

I can never escape from your Spirit!
I can never get away from your presence!
If I go up to heaven, you are there;
if I go down to the grave, you are there.
If I ride the wings of the morning,
if I dwell by the farthest oceans,
even there your hand will guide me,
and your strength will support me.

—Psalm 139:7–10 NLT

In 1905, Charles Hutchinson Gabriel wrote a hymn about the worth and glory of God's presence. I remember holding a hymnal as a young girl in church and watching the faces of the grown-ups around me. They sang the words of this hymn with passion and conviction, clearly moved by the thought of God's nearness.

> I stand amazed in the presence
> Of Jesus the Nazarene,
> And wonder how he could love me,
> A sinner, condemned, unclean.
>
> How marvelous! How wonderful!
> And my song shall ever be;
> How marvelous! How wonderful!
> Is my Savior's love for me![20]

King David wrote a similar song of worship regarding God's presence. Today, during this five-minute practice, find a quiet spot, maybe even in a patch of sunshine, to read all twenty-four verses of Psalm 139. First, read them slowly, soaking up God's presence. Then take a second pass through David's words, making his prayer of worship your own. Your Father stands as a pillar of cloud and a pillar of fire guiding you every step of the way to the promised land.

THIRSTING FOR GOD

If I find in myself desires which nothing in this
world can satisfy, the only logical explanation
is that I was made for another world.
—C. S. LEWIS, *MERE CHRISTIANITY*

I didn't understand thirst until I went two weeks without a single sip of water.

Before that, the longest I'd gone without water had been before a minor outpatient surgery when the nurse instructed me not to eat or drink anything after midnight. Even then, I thought I would die of thirst. Little did I know it could be much worse.

When doctors discovered cancer had returned for the third time, they gave me two weeks to get my affairs in order before my next surgery. This procedure would be much more extensive than the many before, involving a crew of operating room physicians and nurses and a full nine hours to complete. By the time they wheeled me into the recovery room and ICU, my body sported four different surgical wounds—on my leg, arm, and neck and in my mouth. As for the latter, my "new" mouth boasted a live tissue graft pulled from the other areas of my body that would, hopefully, operate as a pseudotongue, allowing me to eat, drink, swallow, and speak, albeit with much difficulty. The seventy-two hours following the surgery were precarious as the surgical team watched to ensure the graft took hold. We needed to make sure the graft survived. So I wasn't allowed even a sip of water or ice chips to quench my thirst.

Two weeks is a long time to go without water. Fourteen days. 336 hours. 20,160 minutes. I'm pretty sure I counted every one. A feeding tube placed directly into my stomach along with an IV allowed nurses to inject fluids and nutrients to keep me alive.

But don't be fooled: "drinking" water through a tube does little to alleviate thirst. It's completely unsatisfying. And does nothing to ease the thick, sandy discomfort of a mouth and throat that have gone dry.

I'll never forget the day the doctor finally gave me the green light to have clear liquids. The first thing I asked for was a glass of cold water. Nothing else. Just water. And although I still couldn't drink or swallow well, I'm not sure I've ever tasted anything so good.

Whenever I read the story of the woman at the well in John 4, I think of those two weeks of maddening thirst. Midday, when the sun burned hottest, this woman went to the community well to draw water. Holy Scripture doesn't reveal her name, but it does reveal ugly parts of her story that she'd likely rather have kept hidden. Of course, in a small town like hers, there's a good chance everyone already knew. Married five times and living with a man who wasn't her husband, she likely wasn't permitted to draw water in the morning along with all the more respectable women.

Jesus sat on the side of the well when she approached. I think He was waiting for her. He knew her story. But rather than pull away, He drew close.

"Will you give me a drink?" He asked (John 4:7). A simple enough request. She was shocked nonetheless.

"You are a Jew and I am a Samaritan woman. How can you ask me for a drink?" (v. 9). Using ethnic divides to distract Him from her moral condition, she addressed the difference in their stations. Jesus was undeterred.

"If you knew the gift of God and who it is that asks you for a drink, you would have asked him and he would have given you living water. . . . Everyone who drinks this water will be thirsty again, but whoever drinks the water I give them will never thirst. Indeed, the water I give them will become in them a spring of water welling up to eternal life" (vv. 10, 13–14).

The woman said, "Sir, give me this water so that I won't get thirsty and have to keep coming here to draw water" (v. 15).

For the next awkward moments, Jesus made it clear that He knew far more about her than she wanted Him to. The defilement of marriage. The pattern of abandoned commitments. The current immoral relationship. He knew all of it. And still He sat within reach. Seeing the thirst behind her behavior, He offered her the one thing she longed for most of all.

Uncomfortable, she did her best to end the conversation. But Jesus was just getting started.

She said, "I know that Messiah . . . is coming. When he comes, he will explain everything to us."

Then Jesus said, "I, the one speaking to you—I am he" (vv. 25–26).

And with that, everything she'd lost was found. Jesus, the Living Water, sat within reach and offered to fill her with Himself.

As author Mark Buchanan says, "Jesus always has food we know nothing about. But he's willing to share."[21] Whether our misguided pursuits involve a string of failed relationships, public rejection, or some other failure, each one of us has made a few bad decisions in our quest to quench our dogged thirst. Time and again, we run to the wrong wells, looking for satisfaction.

Jesus meets us even there. With food and drink we know nothing about. But He's willing to share the full cup of His presence to soothe all that's gone dry inside.

Drink deep, friend, and discover your cup welling up to new life.

Five-Minute Faith Builder

Meanwhile his disciples urged him, "Rabbi, eat something."
But he said to them, "I have food to eat that you know
nothing about."

—JOHN 4:31–32

Are you thirsty? Do you feel as if your soul has gone dry, cracked from circumstances that won't resolve and answers that won't come? Jesus is sitting by your well, waiting to give you Himself. He offers to satisfy your cravings. Will you draw close to Him? Often it's easy to find our way to lesser wells, wells that may even offer temporary relief. I could make a list of these lesser wells, but I'm guessing you already know what one or two of yours are. List them in the margin or in your journal, the wells that promise water but leave you wanting. Name them and offer them to Jesus. Then ask Jesus to satisfy your deepest thirst with the living water of Himself.

DAY 5

WHEN THE WOUNDED WORSHIP

Desire to see God;
Fear to lose Him;
Grieve to be so far from Him;
Rejoice to be brought near Him—
Thus you will live in profound peace.

—TERESA OF AVILA

I sang my first solo in the seventh grade.

Every year, those of us in choir at Parkside Junior High School had the opportunity to participate in a local music competition. It was less about winners and losers, and more about gaining experience. Participants were required to select a song, practice it, and then perform it in front of a panel of judges for a score.

I'd long been terrified of any public performance. Although I'd been a part of children's musicals at our church, I tended to hang back on the fringes, too nervous to risk making a fool of myself in front of a crowd.

But this time, I didn't want to back down. Mrs. Scifres, our choir teacher, asked for volunteers, and I put my hand up. Timid, to be sure, but determined.

"'Edelweiss,'" I told her, once I'd made my music selection. "I want to sing 'Edelweiss.'"

She nodded in agreement, amenable to my *Sound of Music* selection, and I got to work. Weeks later, I stood in front of judges and put my fear to the test. I don't remember my score, not that it mattered. But I do remember this: I did it, and I didn't quit.

That was the first of many solos. For the next twenty-five years, I took singing lessons, eventually singing in college and traveling across the United States in a sponsored college group; I recorded an album (on a cassette tape!); I led worship on Sunday mornings and at retreats, and the list goes on. Using my voice to sing to the God I loved made me feel like I could fly right on home to heaven.

It would not last. By my early forties, cancer came at the cost of two-thirds of my tongue and a mouth and throat burned by radiation. For more than a month during treatment, my vocal cords didn't work at all, too swollen to vibrate and produce sound. I used a dry-erase board to communicate, wondering whether I'd ever be able to speak again, let alone sing.

I would, indeed, sing again. And I'm grateful. But it's not the same. Singing takes extraordinary effort. And although I can sing a verse or two, I often need to take multiple breaks during a three-minute song. Even then, I won't win any competitions. My range is lower, the tone rough. And singing makes my throat hurt, my scarred and stiff vocal cords tired.

Singing now comes at a cost. And barring a miracle, it will for the rest of my life.

I miss it.

Still, last Sunday I sat in the fifth row from the front on the lefthand side, like I do most every Sunday. And while the worship leaders and instrumentalists poured out their worship, I did the same. No holding back, no self-consciousness about the sound of my voice. I sang, loud and proud, regardless of discomfort or quality.

Why?

If I allow myself to grow silent in my suffering, grief wins. But if I sing from the place of my losses, if I turn my face to heaven and praise God for His goodness with a broken voice, then the losses are redeemed in the name of heaven.

And that, my friends, is the most beautiful kind of music. Regardless of how it sounds.

"Through Jesus, therefore, let us continually offer to God a sacrifice of praise—the fruit of lips that openly profess his name" (Heb. 13:15).

What have you lost? What tempts you to shut down your soul and stop singing? Don't let suffering steal your worship. It's not easy, I know. It requires a different kind of courage to step on the stage of your suffering and offer your broken self back to God. But the worship that comes from our wounds is a one-of-a-kind music. And when you do it, you just might find yourself flying right on home to heaven.

Five-Minute Faith Builder

I will sacrifice a freewill offering to you;
*I will praise your name, L*ORD*, for it is good.*
You have delivered me from all my troubles,
and my eyes have looked in triumph on my foes.

—PSALM 54:6–7

The praise that springs from the place of your pain is the most beautiful kind of music. Yes, it's difficult, costly, tender. And yet when you and I choose to worship instead of withdraw, we make room for a love that is greater than any emotion. A love that chooses and not just feels. And a love that pales in comparison with our Father's oceanic love for us. Write down the place of your greatest pain. Use a single word or a date, if you'd like. Doesn't matter. Then read (or sing) the words of Psalm 42 aloud, offering up a sacrifice of praise.

PART 3

THE PRACTICE
OF HUMILITY

Our struggle with faith is often a problem of posture more than pain. Ouch, I know. I don't like writing it any more than you like reading it. But this has proven true in my own life. Somewhere along the way, many of us have come to believe that God owes us. We think that if we work hard to be a good person, we deserve a problem-free, pain-free life. Then when something hard happens, we feel betrayed by the God we trusted to deliver our dreams. It feels personal, punitive. Nothing could be farther from the truth. God has already given us far more than we can ever repay—His *life*. And He never promised us a pain-free existence. He guaranteed the opposite. The practice of humility puts us in the right posture with the one who created us, the one who loves us. On this side of heaven, we will grieve. But He promised that, if we humbly trust Him, He will accomplish a rescue far better than our wildest dreams.

$$\boxed{\text{DAY 1}}$$

SEEING THE REAL ME

*When we see that humility is something infinitely deeper
than contrition, and accept it as our participation in the life
of Jesus, we shall begin to learn that it is our true nobility.*
—ANDREW MURRAY, *HUMILITY*

More than fifteen years after World War II officially came to an end, Adolf Eichmann, a first lieutenant and the SS Nazi mastermind behind the death camps, was captured and put on trial in an Israeli court. The year was 1961, and the shock waves of that horrific war still rippled throughout the world. For many, peace required justice. Thus, many dedicated their lives to tracking and capturing Nazi criminals, including Nazi hunters like Simon Wiesenthal who survived imprisonment in multiple death camps in pursuit of the criminals' prosecution as well as their own peace.

During Eichmann's trial, prosecutors presented a wealth of evidence, including thousands of pages of Eichmann's own words, captured during pretrial interrogation. In addition, they presented the court with a firsthand witness, a man name Yehiel Dinur, a Jewish survivor of one of Eichmann's camps. Dinur's testimony proved a pivotal component of the prosecution's case and, eventually, Eichmann's conviction and death sentence.

In February 1983, twenty-two years after the trial and Dinur's testimony, Mike Wallace interviewed Dinur for an episode of *60 Minutes*.
During the interview, Wallace showed Dinur a video clip of the
Eichmann trial, the moment when Dinur entered the courtroom to
testify. When he entered and saw Eichmann sitting several yards away,
he collapsed to the floor. After the clip ended, Wallace turned to Dinur
and asked him the reason for his collapse. Was it fear? Or hatred?

Neither. Dinur surprised Wallace and viewers with his answer. It
wasn't hate or fear that caused Yehiel Dinur's collapse in the courtroom.
It was Eichmann's ordinariness.

"Eichmann is in all of us," he said, six words that shook all who
heard them. Eichmann wasn't a monster or a fire-breathing dragon.
There was nothing towering or terrifying about him. Instead, he was
average, ordinary. Eichmann appeared no different from the man you
meet on the sidewalk or the stranger you pass at the store. "I was afraid
of myself," said Dinur. "I saw that I am capable to do this. I am . . .
exactly like he." Dinur saw himself.[22]

I'm not sure I'd have the same response. Seldom do I allow myself to
consider the evil I am capable of. It is much easier to see the darkness in
others. Although my flaws are many, I feel the pain of others' infractions
far more than my own. When someone I love fails me, I'm more likely to
feel anger at the wrong than empathy for their struggle. And—dare I say
it?—something dark within even wants to retaliate. Although they hav-
en't committed mass atrocities, I feel compelled to demand vindication for
every wrong. And I doubt the weight of my sin would drop me to the floor.

In the Old Testament book of Exodus sits the familiar story of
Moses delivering the Israelites from slavery in Egypt. Chances are, even
if you are new to Christianity, you're familiar with the story. At last
count, somewhere in the neighborhood of seven movies have been made
about the exodus story, proving that a narrative of unjust suffering and
heroic rescue appeals to a diverse audience, regardless of religious affil-
iation or lack thereof.

Although my early exposure to the exodus story was through simplistic Sunday school lessons, I've since learned the many ways the exodus foreshadows the gospel: a people enslaved by evil, a deliverer sent to rescue, and a promised land waiting for those who are set free. Moses' journey foreshadowed a better salvation, one that would come thousands of years later when Jesus—a name that in Hebrew means "to save"—died on a cross to set those who were enslaved to their flawed humanity free.

But before the exodus, the Israelites faced a final Egyptian plague: the plague of the firstborn (see Exodus 11). In spite of God's persistent warnings to "let my people go," Pharaoh remained unmoved (Ex. 7:15–16). Concerned about His people's suffering and Pharaoh's hardness of heart, God sent an angel of death to wipe out every firstborn male, both people and livestock. A devastating blow against evil. But this is what I want you to notice: the plague was to wipe out every firstborn male, Egyptian and Israelite alike.

But God offered the Israelites an out. Each family was to slaughter a single, perfect male lamb. Then they were to take some of the blood and put it on the sides and tops of their door frames. That night, the angel of death would deliver the final judgment but pass over and spare Israelite homes covered by the blood of the lamb.

Sound familiar? Thousands of years later, another Lamb's blood was offered for anyone who receives its cover. Even so, we mustn't forget: Egypt is in all of us. The Israelites were destined for death as well as their slave drivers. The only difference, their only salvation, was the blood of the lamb.

Theologian and Yale professor Miroslav Volf, a Croatian who has witnessed humanity's propensity to see evil everywhere but in oneself, concludes, "Forgiveness flounders because I exclude the enemy from the community of humans even as I exclude myself from the community of sinners. . . . When one knows [as the cross demonstrates] that the torturer will not eternally triumph over the victim, one is free to rediscover that person's humanity and imitate God's love for him. And when one knows [as the cross demonstrates] that God's love is greater than all sin, one is free to see oneself in the light of God's justice and so rediscover one's own sinfulness."[23]

Yes, Eichmann and Egypt are in all of us. The only salvation for humankind, including both you and me, is to be covered by the blood of the Lamb.

Five-Minute Faith Builder

Blessed are the poor in spirit, for theirs is the kingdom of heaven.

—MATTHEW 5:3

In a culture that spends so much time and money talking about self-esteem, the practice of humility is severely neglected. Desperate to feel good about ourselves, we'd rather stay blind to our sin. As a result, we remain slaves. If you're physically able, spend a few moments on your knees in prayer. First, look at yourself with as much clarity and honesty as you can muster. Don't try to make yourself feel better; don't attempt to downplay your sinfulness or need. Tell the truth and own it. Then after facing your flawed self, picture Jesus covering you with Himself. Pray this prayer:

Jesus, I don't deserve Your deliverance, but I receive it. Thank You for saving me.

No more slavery and shame, friend. Only freedom.

$$\boxed{\text{DAY 2}}$$

NO EXCUSES

Humility . . . is stark, raving honesty. We cannot receive
what the crucified Rabbi has to give unless we admit our
plight and stretch out our hands until our arms ache.
—Brennan Manning, *The Rabbi's Heart*

If ever you doubt humanity's propensity to deny responsibility, you need look no farther than my three teenaged children.

Why didn't you put your dishes in the dishwasher? You didn't tell me to.

Why did you punch your sister? She was being annoying.

Why didn't you turn in your homework? The teacher didn't remind me.

I could fill up a full page with the examples of deflected responsibility I've heard in the past week alone. We humans love making excuses, my children included.

To capture our tendency to shift blame, late cartoonist Bil Keane in his popular comic strip, *Family Circus*, introduced an invisible character called Not Me. *Family Circus* (which debuted in 1960 and continues in production to this day) depicts the daily life of two parents and their four children. Again and again, when asked who did a misdeed, the children deflect blame by stating, "Not me." Thus, the birth of the imaginary character.

Although I'm loath to admit it, I'm not much better. It's easier to make excuses than to look hard at the self. After all, who enjoys surgery? Much easier to direct the knife elsewhere.

And yet without honesty there cannot be health. As pastor and author Brennan Manning said, "Whatever is denied cannot be healed. . . . Peace lies in acceptance of truth."[24] That means that instead of a defensive "Not me!" we need to own it: "Ugh, that's me."

Why does this matter in the life of faith? Faith, by definition, demands trusting in something outside of oneself. But until we stop making excuses, we'll never see our need for anything or anyone but ourselves. Self-sufficiency has no need of faith.

King Solomon recognized the wisdom of God's correction and our confession: "My child, don't reject the LORD's discipline, and don't be upset when he corrects you. For the LORD corrects those he loves, just as a father corrects a child in whom he delights" (Prov. 3:11–12 NLT). And the author of Hebrews acknowledged the long-term benefit of God's discipline: "No discipline is enjoyable while it is happening—it's painful! But afterward there will be a peaceful harvest of right living for those who are trained in this way" (Heb. 12:11 NLT).

A powerful illustration of this truth is seen in Peter's and Judas's different responses to failure on the night of Jesus' arrest. Judas betrayed Jesus to the spiritual leaders in exchange for some silver, eventually leading them to the garden of Gethsemane, where they arrested Him. Peter, after Jesus' arrest, denied knowing Him three separate times to avoid a similar fate. Both chose to turn their backs on the man they had previously called friend. Peter, though, ended up a pivotal leader in the church after the resurrection. And Judas ended up alone and committed suicide.

What made the difference? What led one man to spiritual transformation while the other ended up in spiritual devastation?

Peter did more than experience regret. Upon hearing the rooster crow, he remembered Jesus' painful prediction, and with a spiritual knife, he faced his truest self. What he discovered devastated him. But it did not isolate him. Peter's honest reflection led him to return to Jesus. And this is where Judas's story took a fork in the road. Judas may have experienced regret, but he didn't return to his Savior. As Manning says, "Accepting the reality of our sinfulness means accepting our authentic self. Judas could not face his shadow; Peter could. The latter befriended the imposter within; the former raged against him."[25]

While excuses lead to isolation, confession facilitates connection, with both God and others. But first we need to face our true self. Pride wants to be right; humility admits we're often wrong. Pride wants to dominate; humility wants to relate. Although pride eventually brings us down, humility ultimately raises us up. South African writer and pastor Andrew Murray, makes it clear: "The truth is this: Pride may die in you, or nothing of heaven can live in you."[26]

"So humble yourselves under the mighty power of God," Peter wrote near the end of his life, "and at the right time he will lift you up in honor" (1 Peter 5:6 NLT).

If you and I want to live full of faith in the one who holds the power to redeem our biggest regrets, we must, like Peter, have the courage to face our true selves, without excuse. Grace can reach only for those who know they need it. No more "Not me." Only a humble life that returns to the Savior.

Five-Minute Faith Builder

For I know my transgressions,
  and my sin is always before me.
Against you, you only, have I sinned
  and done what is evil in your sight;
so you are right in your verdict
  and justified when you judge.

—PSALM 51:3–4

Although I've lived several decades, the same weaknesses continue to plague me. You too? You're in good company. Here's an important question for both of us: When we fail, does our grief over our sin lead us *to* Jesus or away from Him? Are we more dependent on Him or less so? Defensiveness creates distance, but confession creates connection. Trust that Jesus doesn't want to berate you, He wants to build you. Don't waste any more time hiding behind excuses and blame. Instead, draw near. Today, take stock of your regrets. Write them down in your journal or in the margin. Then ask yourself, Do I own these mistakes? Or make excuses for them? Do I bring them to Jesus? Or deny them? Spend a few minutes telling God the truth. It's okay. He loves you anyway.

DAY 3

THE FREEDOM OF CONFESSION

In confession occurs the breakthrough of the cross.
—DIETRICH BONHOEFFER, *LIFE TOGETHER*

If I were to make a list of my childhood entertainment, the list wouldn't include cell phones, Netflix, Minecraft, or reality TV. They didn't exist yet. I was about seventeen when we got our first VCR. (And what is a VCR, you ask? A video cassette recorder. You're welcome.) Soon after, we acquired a large collection of VHS tapes. (And what is a VHS tape, you wonder? A video home system tape roughly the size and weight of a hefty library book.) Our collection was predominantly of Disney movies like *The Little Mermaid* and *The Great Mouse Detective*, and their bulky plastic cases took up an entire entertainment-center cabinet. What a wonder! We were on the cutting edge of all cutting edges, the pinnacle of human innovation and achievement!

I donated all of those VHS tapes several summers ago. I'm confident the eighteen-year-old who received the donation didn't have a clue what they were.

In addition to VCRs and VHS tapes, my childhood entertainment included things like Rubik's Cube (which is making a comeback!), a Merlin electronic game, and a collection of Smurf figurines. But you know what was the best part of my childhood entertainment? 1970s and '80s sitcoms. *M*A*S*H*, *The Dukes of Hazzard*, *Laverne & Shirley*, and *Scooby-Doo*. (The original *Scooby-Doo*. Scrappy was a sad, sad turn in the Scooby-verse.) Perhaps the best of the bunch? The one and only *Happy Days*.

Starring a youthful Ron Howard, *Happy Days* showcased the ordinary lives of a group of teenagers who often hung out at a diner named Happy Days. From 1974 to 1984, *Happy Days* entertained audiences with a total of 255 episodes. But perhaps the most memorable scenes from all of them are the ones in which Fonzie, the handsome leather-wearing biker character, did something wrong and needed to apologize. For all his bravado, he couldn't do it.

"I was wrorrrrr . . ." he'd try. "It was my faaaurrrrr . . ." No matter his effort, he couldn't get the words to come out.

"I'm sorrrrr . . ." Nope, not that one either.

Without ownership and public confession, Fonzie's relationships remained strained. His pride mattered more to him than his people. Confession, although painful, would bring him to a place of humility and make possible the restoration of relationship. But he first needed to get over the enormous hurdle of his ego.

When it comes to confession of sin, big or small, I can think of no greater example than in the life of Brother Lawrence of the Resurrection. A seventeenth-century Carmelite lay-brother, he made his entire life about living moment by moment in God's presence. *The Practice of the Presence of God*, a collection of his letters and insights, is a go-to resource when I need to revisit humility and confession. Although Brother Lawrence served as cook in his monastery, he considered "practicing" God's presence with him to be his true vocation.

Part of that practice included regularly confessing sin, whether it be a wayward thought or a selfish attitude. When he sinned, he confessed it to God with these simple words: "I can do nothing better without You. Please keep me from falling and correct the mistakes I make." Aware of his sins and not surprised by them, he stated, "That is my nature, the only thing I know how to do." And if he didn't sin, he gave thanks for it, knowing it was God's grace alone that protected him from himself.[27]

Simple? Yes. Easy? No. Confession is counterintuitive. Instinct makes us want to hide our mistakes beneath a veneer of confidence, a dual effort to save face and relationship. We don't want to be embarrassed and humiliated in front of our friends. And yet when we refuse admission, we end up alone in our cover-up.

Thank heavens, the author of Hebrews offers a white flag: "For we do not have a high priest who is unable to empathize with our weaknesses, but we have one who has been tempted in every way, just as we are—yet he did not sin. Let us then approach God's throne of grace with confidence, so that we may receive mercy and find grace to help us in our time of need" (Heb. 4:15–16).

Ours is a God who is compassionate toward our human predicament and gives us courage in our confession. This is true freedom, with God and each other. In the process, we discover deeper and more authentic relationship. And maybe even happy days.

Five-Minute Faith Builder

But who can discern their own errors?
Forgive my hidden faults.

—PSALM 19:12

On a scale of 1 to 10, with 1 representing being like Fonzie and 10 representing being like Brother Lawrence, how comfortable are you with confession? How readily do you say "I'm sorry" and "I was wrong," even when no one demands that you do it? Spend a few moments asking God to reveal to you where you need to practice confession. Then scan Nehemiah chapters 9 and 10. When the Israelites returned to Jerusalem and rebuilt her walls, they recognized how far they'd strayed from God's law and their need to confess their failure. Nehemiah 9 reveals their process of confession, and Nehemiah 10 details their plan of repentance. Note anything you learn, and then consider how you might apply these insights. Remember: confession is the path to connection. Don't be afraid. God's grace is ready.

DAY 4

HUMILITY'S POSTURE

*To live by grace means to acknowledge my whole life
story, the light side and the dark. In admitting my shadow
side I learn who I am and what God's grace means.
As Thomas Merton put it, "A saint is not someone who
is good but who experiences the goodness of God."*
—BRENNAN MANNING, *THE RAGAMUFFIN GOSPEL*

He was angry. That much was obvious. Even from my seat on the airport parking shuttle, I could see the man's clenched jaw and seething eyes. I glanced at the shuttle driver, who was standing at the door, and back at the man, who was standing on the curb next to his wife and surrounded by his luggage. I felt a sting of empathy for my driver because of the tongue-lashing he was about to receive.

"I'm sorry, sir," he said from the open shuttle door. "I don't have any more room. The next shuttle will be here in a few moments."

The man wasn't having it.

"Are you serious?! You were supposed to pick us up over there." He pointed twenty yards away to a space occupied by two other airport shuttles. "That's where I was standing." His fury oozed. I wanted to crawl into a hole and I wasn't even the object of his ire.

The shuttle driver attempted, yet again, to apologize.

"I'm sorry, sir. There was another bus there. I came as close as I could."

The man refused to back down.

"That's a lie. There wasn't anyone there." His voice continued to crescendo, as if he could make two empty seats appear on the shuttle by ratcheting up his volume. "I'm calling your manager. I guess you don't value your job."

Once again, our driver could only apologize. "I'm sorry, sir. Another shuttle is around the corner." He tried to show his would-be passenger the overstuffed luggage racks, but it didn't matter. There would be no mercy for him today.

When the shuttle doors closed, I breathed a sigh of relief, along with my fellow passengers. None of us wanted to share a fifteen-minute ride with that man or his anger. We did our best to encourage our driver, but the damage was done.

A few weeks ago, I read these words and have been thinking about them ever since: "Remind the people to be subject to rulers and authorities, to be obedient, to be ready to do whatever is good, to slander no one, to be peaceable and considerate, and *always to be gentle toward everyone*" (Titus 3:1–2, emphasis mine).

"Be gentle toward everyone," Paul wrote to Titus in a letter intended to offer mentoring to a young man following in his ministry footsteps. Whether we're preaching behind a podium or standing on an airport curb waiting for a ride, Paul reminds us that gentleness isn't something to occasionally pull out of our pockets and use when it's convenient. It isn't only for when we feel like it or for those who deserve it.

Be gentle toward everyone. Always. Hard stop.

This is difficult for me. Why? Well, for starters, gentleness doesn't come naturally to me. Decisiveness? Determination? Grit? All of the above, without much effort. But gentleness? Not so much.

And second, well—how should I say it?—some people are

ridiculous. (I told you gentleness isn't my jam.) They do dumb stuff and act foolishly and behave in ways that warrant anything but a gentle hand. Humans are so very *human*. And some days I don't want to be gentle. I want to slap them upside the head and give them a good yelling.

Case in point, the man at the airport.

But then Paul's letter to Titus, his command to "always be gentle." Right after those words, Paul gives us the reason why: "At one time we too were foolish" (v. 3).

Me? Foolish? Surely not.

Alas, yes. More than once (this week). I misspoke, misbehaved, and acted in ways that deserved anything but gentleness. I've been petty and impatient with strangers, friends, coworkers, family members. I've even been petty and impatient with my ever-patient God. Foolish? In spades.

"But when the kindness and love of God our Savior appeared, he saved us, not because of righteous things we had done, but because of his mercy" (vv. 4–5).

Because of his mercy.

Jesus didn't wait for me to earn it, deserve it, or prove my worthiness of it. He was gentle and kind and merciful because it is His nature to be so. His gentleness isn't because of my character but because of His.

There will be times when our words need to be firm, direct, candid. There will be people and situations that require bold confrontation. But boldness and gentleness can work well together.

This call to gentleness isn't a call to playing the doormat.

It is a call to a posture.

It's a gentleness sourced in humility, one that fully understands what it feels like to be the fool who received a mercy he didn't deserve. And one that longs to deliver that same mercy to as many fools as need it in return.

Dallas Willard knocks the knees out from under any of us who feel we sit closer to God's ear than any other as a result of our merits: "When God speaks to us, it does not prove that we are righteous or even right.

It does not even prove that we have correctly understood what he said. The infallibility of the messenger and the message does not guarantee the infallibility of our reception. Humility is always in order."[28]

Humility recognizes that any ability to approach God is a result of mercy, not merit. It knows to its core that you and I don't deserve kindness or gentleness or grace any more than the ridiculous person next to us, on the shuttle or on the curb. But nevertheless, we have received it.

Take stock of your posture today, friends. We're standing in an ocean of grace we don't deserve. Let's offer the gentleness of humility to whoever we find here.

Five-Minute Faith Builder

Instead, whoever wants to become great among you must be your servant, and whoever wants to be first must be your slave.

—MATTHEW 20:26–27

Although Jesus was God, He chose a posture of humility, both in taking on human form and in His attitudes and actions. Although He was and is Lord and King, He chose servanthood and sacrifice, for our sakes. Philippians 2 describes this shocking contrast between Jesus' God-ness and His willing lowness, a posture Paul tells us to emulate. Read all thirty verses of Philippians 2. After reading it one time, go back and highlight any evidence you see of humility. Then turn that evidence into a short, bulleted list describing the person who exhibits humility. Consider your own life. What is one action you can take to assume a posture of humility today?

DAY 5

THE REFUGE OF MERCY

*Only two things have ever changed the
human soul: the fall and grace.*
—Dr. Larry Crabb, *Connecting*

I saw her petite profile in the mirror while my hairstylist worked magic on my hair. She wore a gray crown of thinning glory, skin weathered by time, with a perfect taupe handbag clutched neatly in her lap. While her stylist styled her gray in a chair right behind me, my stylist tried to cover mine up. Something that requires more and more time and hair product. But I digress.

I guessed her to be somewhere near eighty years old. She was still going to the salon to get her hair done, much as my grandmother did most of her life. Back then, women scheduled a standing weekly salon appointment during which their stylists washed and curled their hair to beatific glory. No self-respecting woman missed her weekly hair appointment.

About the time my graying crown had been covered with enough foil to communicate with alien life forms, something changed. Because I was facing the opposite direction, I looked in the mirror to figure out what was happening behind me. But all I could see was the stylist helping the older woman stand and walk to the back of the store.

That's when I noticed the smell. After early years working in the nursing field and the following years raising children, I knew what had happened: She'd had an accident. A bad one. Right there, fully clothed and in the middle of a hair salon.

I felt an automatic reaction to the overpowering odor and its implication. But I didn't want to cover my nose, turn my head, do anything to add to the woman's humiliation. One thing alone kept me from reacting: not long before, I'd done something similar. I'll spare you the details, but trust me when I say it was, hands down, one of the most humiliating experiences of my life. For months I'd been bedridden and then hospital bound from the cumulative impact of chemotherapy and radiation. And although I was a young mom with round-the-clock care, my body was shutting down and I could no longer control basic functions. And the humiliation of it all filled me with shame.

That day, as I sat in my stylist's chair with a foiled head, I felt the woman's humiliation. An hour before, she'd left her home to get her hair done, something that should have made her feel beautiful. Instead, shame swallowed up her significance somewhere between her salon chair and the bathroom door.

I closed my eyes and prayed, for the woman as well as her stylist, who graciously walked her to the restroom and helped her clean herself up. It made me think of the nurse who did the same for me, preserving remnants of my dignity by offering mercy. A gift I'll never forget.

Every day we run into people in dignity-stealing situations. The homeless man on the corner. The Alzheimer's patient who can't remember her first name. The teenager eight months pregnant. The elderly gentleman who asks you to repeat yourself a half dozen times because he can't hear. The chemo-sick woman with a scarf wrapped around her bald head.

In every case, shame steals significance.

Let's steal it back. The difference between humiliation and humility is often the simple gift of mercy. Humility allows us to stoop into the

75

shameful circumstance of the suffering, because we recognize it could just as easily be us in the same position. Although we may feel tempted to cringe or pull away, we can practice a mercy response. It may be uncomfortable, and often we'll experience a measure of suffering when we step into another's. But isn't that what Mercy has done for us?

Early in the Old Testament, God gave Joshua, the leader of the Israelites, a strange command: "Tell the Israelites to designate the cities of refuge" (Josh. 20:2; see also Numbers 35; Deuteronomy 4; Deuteronomy 19).

In all, there were six cities of refuge. These cities were places where lawbreakers could flee and find safety. During that time, the law required an accounting for every mistake, as well as consequences for every mistaker. But the six cities of refuge allowed for mercy. Without going into detail, this is what you need to know about these cities:

First, if someone accidentally murdered another, the nearest male relative of the man murdered, called the avenger of blood, was permitted to avenge his relative's death. Eye for an eye and all that.

Second, the accused could flee to the city of refuge, but he needed to reach the city gate, the typical place for legal proceedings, before the avenger found him.

And finally, after pleading his case, the accused would be required to stay in the city of refuge until the death of the high priest. This was intended to limit the punishment of the guilty.

Now read that one more time. Do you see the implications?

God the Father is the ultimate avenger of blood, the only one truly justified to make us pay: "For we know him who said, 'It is mine to avenge; I will repay,' and again, 'The Lord will judge his people.' It is a dreadful thing to fall into the hands of the living God" (Heb. 10:30–31).

But not one of us would survive a trial. So God the Father sent Jesus. We need only to run to him to find mercy: "I am the gate; whoever enters through me will be saved. They will come in and go out, and find pasture" (John 10:9).

When would we be free, our sins and fear of death be removed? When the reigning high priest died.

"Jesus said, 'It is finished.' With that, he bowed his head and gave up his spirit" (John 19:30).

Although God had every right to exact a price from those of us who broke the law, He provided us a city of refuge, Emmanuel, God with Us, so we would always, always have somewhere to run and be safe.

"It is not sin that humbles most, but grace," Andrew Murray said.[29] And when you and I grasp the magnitude of mercy we have received, we'll begin to live as cities of refuge for others, safe places where the humiliated and hurting can flee and find the refuge of Jesus too.

Five-Minute Faith Builder

Have mercy on me, my God, have mercy on me,
for in you I take refuge.
I will take refuge in the shadow of your wings
until the disaster has passed.

—PSALM 57:1

Jesus is our entry into God's mercy, the city of refuge to which we can flee and find grace. What does this mean to you personally? Where do you most need mercy right now? Psalm 57:1 says, "Have mercy on me, my God, have mercy on me, for in you I take refuge. I will take refuge in the shadow of your wings until the disaster has passed." Are you taking refuge under the merciful arms of God? If so, how can you practice humility by offering a refuge of mercy to someone else who needs it?

PART 4

THE PRACTICE OF RELINQUISHMENT

If there is one thing we crave, it is control. We want power, agency, the ability to steer circumstances and people in a desired direction. Behind our control-freak tendencies, though, sits fear. We are wired to see and avoid danger. So we exert control in an effort to preserve life. Problem is, life refuses to be contained, and it remains riddled with danger regardless of our attempts to avoid it. Sooner or later, when the unexpected wrecks us, we must face the truth of how little we can control.

Hebrews 11 says, "The fundamental fact of existence is that this trust in God, this faith, is the firm foundation under everything that makes life worth living" (vv. 1–2 MSG). Faith in our ability to control eventually leads to disappointment. But faith in God's control? That's the foundation that secures our lives, no matter what happens. Time to relinquish control to the only one who can hold it all together.

$$\boxed{\text{DAY 1}}$$

THE NEVER-ENDING DRIVE FOR CONTROL

One of the hardest things to decide during a dark night is whether to surrender or resist. The choice often comes down to what you believe about God and how God acts, which means that every dark night of the soul involves wrestling with belief.
—BARBARA BROWN TAYLOR,
LEARNING TO WALK IN THE DARK

Rain poured down in sheets outside my passenger seat window, continuing as it had been for hours. Rain isn't uncommon in middle Tennessee, but this was a torrential rain. Pushing up from the Gulf of Mexico, a tropical system spread across the state in an ominous wave of thunderstorms, leaving swollen rivers and saturated yards in its wake. My driver, Kyle, kept both hands firmly on the steering wheel, which I appreciated.

In spite of the rain, traffic on I-65 continued at a steady pace. Rush hour in Nashville is known for its congested traffic, and this day was no exception. I glanced at my watch to check the time. I still had well over an hour until my plane departed to take me back home. Plenty of time to check my luggage and get to my gate, thanks to TSA precheck.

What happened next is difficult to piece together. In the span of seconds, Kyle and I watched as the car in front of us hydroplaned on the highway and then ricocheted off a semitrailer truck before spinning out in the direction of our car. Kyle, again with two expert hands on the steering wheel, pressed the brake and maneuvered to the right to miss the spinning sedan, while simultaneously avoiding the other cars traveling sixty-five miles per hour in parallel lanes.

It all happened in less than thirty seconds. I still have no idea how he avoided a collision. Breathless, Kyle pulled onto the shoulder in front of the unmoving white sedan. We sat there stunned. Then we turned to look at the car behind us.

Oh no. The car was crushed on the driver's side, airbags deployed and blocking our view of any passengers. I couldn't imagine how anyone inside survived without injury. And yet seconds later, while we walked in the rain toward the white car, I watched as the driver, a young woman in her twenties, crawled through the front passenger door to stand in the rain with us. Shaken, but unharmed.

"Are you okay?" Kyle and I asked in unison.

"Yes, I think so," she said. We looked her over to be sure. No blood, no visible broken bones. A scraped and tender right arm, likely from the airbag. But that was it. I couldn't believe it. What a miracle.

"Thank heavens you were wearing your seat belt," I exhaled.

That's when she stunned me more than the accident itself did.

"I wasn't."

I grew up in a time when seat belts were optional. I remember multiday family road trips across the United States during which my brother and I turned the back seat of our parents' Oldsmobile into something of a playground. There wasn't a seat belt to be found.

But plenty of research has since been done to prove the lifesaving worth of a seat belt. No matter how many years of experience we have, no matter how skilled we are at driving, we can't control every variable, including weather, road conditions, and other drivers. We have a choice: Either we can gamble and forego the seat belt, hoping everything goes according to plan. That's a bit like playing Russian roulette with a semi while hydroplaning on a Tennessee highway during a rainstorm. Or we can put our trust in something stronger that can hold us firm when the unexpected happens. A seat belt. I highly recommend the latter.

The same is true for the life of faith. It all comes down to how we answer two questions:

1. Do I believe my life is at risk from unexpected circumstances?
2. Do I believe, if and when the unexpected happens, God has the power to hold me firm?

None of us escapes this life unscathed. Sooner or later, every single one of us will end up in a grave. The only question is, In who or what will I put my trust to save me on that day?

Whether we're trusting our own efforts, blind luck, or God, we're putting all of our eggs in one basket. But only one basket is strong enough to hold all of our eggs. "Come to me, all you who are weary and burdened, and I will give you rest," Jesus said. "Take my yoke upon you and learn from me, for I am gentle and humble in heart, and you will find rest for your souls. For my yoke is easy and my burden is light" (Matt. 11:28–30).

Yes, please wear a seat belt. It's smart, and it could save your life. But never forget: the ultimate safety we're searching for can be found only in relinquishing control to the one worthy of holding it.

Jesus. He is the one to trust, even when the storms rage. Especially then.

Five-Minute Faith Builder

At that time the disciples came to Jesus and asked, "Who, then, is the greatest in the kingdom of heaven?" He called a little child to him, and placed the child among them. And he said: "Truly I tell you, unless you change and become like little children, you will never enter the kingdom of heaven."

—MATTHEW 18:1–3

Anyone here a bit of a control freak? Trust me when I say both of my hands are way up. Here's a hard question: Where do you find yourself trying to take control? If you're not sure, take a look at what you're afraid of. The things you fear losing are often tied to what you over-control. If you fear most for your children, you will control them and the people who have contact with them. If you fear running out of money, you will over-control your finances. If you fear being abandoned or alone, you might find yourself exercising too much control in your relationships, even if that means staying safely detached. Make a list of the areas in which you find yourself attempting control. Then open your hands, palms up, and pray, "I relinquish _____ to you, God. You are the one I trust."

┌─────────────┐
│   **DAY 2**   │
└─────────────┘

THE RELIEF OF LETTING GO

*If you love anything at all in this world more than God,
you will crush that object under the weight of your
expectations, and it will eventually break your heart.*
—TIMOTHY KELLER, PRAYER

For as long as I can remember, I dreamed of being a mother. I pictured a house full of children, family holidays filled with laughter and traditions, photo albums filled with school pictures, family vacations, and momentous events. This desire influenced where I chose to attend college and how I built a career. I didn't want anything to get in the way of my dreams of family. Which is in large part why finding out I had cancer while I still had young children at home wrecked me. I looked at my children and couldn't bear the thought of missing out on their lives.

What pained me the most, though, was the very real possibility that I could die, and then someone else would take my place as my children's mother. I didn't want anyone else to play wife to my husband or mom to my children. That was *my* job. And the fact that I might not be around to fulfill it haunted me. As a result, I tried to hang on to them more tightly. Of course, the tighter you cling to people, the more they resent it. What felt like love to me felt like a stranglehold to them.

This is often the case with more than just people. Try to grasp love, and you'll lose it. Reach for affirmation and attention, and they will remain elusive. Try to seek financial success, and you'll miss out on it. Hold it all loosely, though, and you just might find what you were looking for.

In 1857, a twenty-year-old businessman surrendered to God. Although not rich by human standards, he had a solid head for business and desired success. But on his twentieth birthday, he came to a deep awareness of God's reality and determined to surrender it all to Him, including his dreams of personal and financial success.

On that particular day, Thomas Maclellan penned a prayer releasing his dreams and plans to the will of Christ. This radical relinquishment is difficult to do at any stage in life, even for those who have followed Jesus for decades. But it's hard to imagine a twenty-year-old aspiring businessman releasing his future and pending success so fully into the hands of his God. And yet this is what Thomas Maclellan did.

"To Thy direction also, I resign myself and all that I have to be disposed of by Thee as Thou shalt see fit. To Thee I leave the management of all events and desire that Thou enable me to say, without reserve, not my will but Thine be done. Knowing that Thou governest all things wisely and will ever do that which is best for me."[30] This is only a small section of the covenant he penned. But it provides a glimpse of his relinquishment of those things he would, otherwise, be tempted to cling to.

Fast-forward more than a hundred and fifty years and Thomas's covenantal prayer has multiplied into the Maclellan Foundation and more than $600 million in total donations. One man's willingness to give himself to the will of God has now become generations of men, women, and dollars reinvested in the kingdom. All because one man was willing to let go.[31]

There's a story told in the gospel books of Mark and Luke about a poor widow who came to the temple to give her offering (Mark 12:41–44; Luke 21:1–4). Moments before, Jesus had issued a warning against the teachers of the law, blasting them for their displays of religiosity while "devour[ing] widows' houses." They aimed for fame, grasping for attention and recognition. But they failed to see those who needed them most of all.

Against that backdrop, a widow entered the temple along with a crowd of worshipers with offerings. Many deposited huge sums, making quite a show with the sound of their gifts. But the widow offered a couple of coins, an amount so small that no one noticed. Her contribution couldn't possibly make a difference. It was less than nothing.

Jesus noticed: "Truly I tell you, this poor widow has put more into the treasury than all the others. They all gave out of their wealth; but she, out of her poverty, put in everything—all she had to live on" (Mark 12:43–44).

Whether your gift is money or ministry, it is possible to give large amounts without giving anything at all. And it is possible to give little and yet give everything. The widow did what so many others find difficult: she held nothing back. Proving that God Himself was indeed her truest treasure, she relinquished all of her earthly riches. And in the end, she left far richer than the rest.

This is the gift of letting go, of relinquishing all we have, even our lives, to a God who sees. Your sacrifice matters, no matter how big or small. Trust Him with it and watch as your faith grows in the giving.

Five-Minute Faith Builder

*I have been crucified with Christ and I no longer live,
but Christ lives in me. The life I now live in the body, I
live by faith in the Son of God, who loved me and gave
himself for me.*

—GALATIANS 2:20

Much like the widow with her two coins, Thomas Maclellan relinquished his life to his God in a prayer on his twentieth birthday. "Consecrate all that I am and all that I have, the faculties of my mind, the members of my body, my worldly possessions, my time, and my influence over others, all to be used entirely for Thy glory and resolutely employed in obedience to Thy commands as long as Thou continuest me in life."[32] Read this section of his prayer one more time, and highlight any words or phrases that are meaningful to you. Then find a quiet place, absent of distraction, and pray Thomas's prayer aloud, releasing your life into the hands of the God who loves you more than all others. "To him who is able to keep you from stumbling and to present you before his glorious presence without fault and with great joy" (Jude 24).

$$\boxed{\text{DAY 3}}$$

OPENHANDED LIVING

I also believe that many a man is praying to God to
fill him, when he is full already with something else.
Before we pray that God would fill us, I believe we
ought to pray that He would empty us. There must be
an emptying before there can be a filling; and when
the heart is turned upside down, and everything that is
contrary to God is turned out, then the Spirit will come.

—DWIGHT L. MOODY

I started a new workout a few months ago called the Lagree Fitness Method. It is similar to Pilates, but more challenging. Through a series of slow and repetitive movements on a compact machine called the Megaformer, Lagree focuses on strengthening short muscle fibers without damaging connective tissue. Low impact but high intensity, Lagree is helping me build my core and upper-body strength, along with my legs. Movements are slow, constant, and at times brutal in their difficulty. It requires incredible mental discipline to stay engaged rather than tap out. Even so, I love it. And at my age, I know this strength building is essential for my overall health, agility, and longevity.

Often during Lagree, my instructor reminds me to "watch for

shoulder creep" and "keep a loose grip on the handles." As the intensity (and pain) of the workout increases, so does my grip. Often during the course of the fifty-minute class, I find my shoulders bunched up by my ears and my hands wrapped in a death grip around the handles. The challenge of the exercises causes me to tense up and tighten my hold. The irony is that this diverts attention away from the muscles that need to grow in strength. The moment I loosen my grip, I feel my legs and core grow stronger.

Relinquishing my hold produces better results.

The same is true for the journey of faith. Often when challenges mount, we respond by doubling down and holding even more tightly to the things and people we love most. We imagine ourselves in control, able to bend circumstances and people to our desires.

But a tighter grip won't deliver what we want.

The only way you and I can loosen our hands' grip on the temporal things of life is to hold on to Jesus most of all. When He is the object of our greatest affection, we can release the other parts of our lives to Him. And when we loosen our grip on lesser loves, we will discover a new core strength.

Brother Lawrence, the Carmelite monk I mentioned in the practice of confession, learned how to live openhandedly in the presence of God. A friend later wrote the following about Brother Lawrence: "The worst trial he could imagine was losing his sense of God's presence, which had been with him for so long a time. However, his confidence in God's goodness made him certain that He would never leave him entirely. Should he encounter any great difficulty in his life, he knew the Lord would provide the strength he needed to endure it. With this assurance, Brother Lawrence wasn't afraid of anything. He added that he wasn't afraid of dying to self or losing himself in Christ, because complete surrender to God's will is the only secure road to follow. In it there is always enough light to assure safe travel."[33]

Although he never achieved worldly success, Brother Lawrence achieved something few of us ever experience: the peace of openhanded living. As a result, he felt extraordinary joy in the ordinariness of his daily life. Although his life was not without challenges, he found his peace uninterrupted simply because he held onto what mattered most of all: God Himself.

Five-Minute Faith Builder

Trust in the LORD with all your heart
and lean not on your own understanding;
in all your ways submit to him,
and he will make your paths straight.

—PROVERBS 3:5–6

Part of Brother Lawrence's experience of God's presence included the regular practice of surrender. When he felt himself stray from God's presence because of some distraction or even sin, he immediately turned his face toward God with an expression of affection: "My God, I am all Yours; do what You will with me."[34] Baked into these words sits a confidence in God's perfect love, and a belief that God will never act outside of that perfect love. Thus, surrender brings no panic. What is there to fear when surrendering to Love? For today's Five-Minute Faith Builder, close your eyes and pray Brother Lawrence's prayer: "My God, I am all Yours; do what You will with me." Repeat this prayer five times slowly, releasing your worries and concerns with open hands to the one who loves you most of all.

DAY 4

TRUST WITHOUT GUARANTEES OR CONDITIONS

They have a holy stubbornness, like Job. They keep believing that someday, God will show up and explain it all, or maybe show up and refuse to explain any of it but make it all okay anyhow.
—MARK BUCHANAN, SPIRITUAL RHYTHM

It's one thing to dream about a home renovation. It's another thing to survive the reality of it.

As a general contractor for the past twenty years, Troy often observes the painful disconnect between a customer's dream and a project's reality. Although it's dubbed reality TV, HGTV tells only a thirty-minute version of the real story. At first, homeowners love renovation. But a couple of weeks in, the glow of the dream turns into the gutting of demolition. When renovation becomes a mess—and all renovations do—the excitement ebbs and the most optimistic HGTVer doubts their decision.

Remodel my house, they say. But keep the noise down. Renovate my kitchen, but don't create any dust. Build me a custom-finished basement with a high-end theater room and all the bells and whistles, but don't spend much money.

Although they want a beautiful result, trust comes with conditions, understandably so. And while that makes sense when hiring a general contractor to do a specific job, the same cannot be done on the journey of faith.

When it comes to our relationship with God, trust with demands isn't really trust at all. It's merely a transaction. And God isn't in the business of a work-for-hire relationship. I doubt that's really what we need or want anyway. Even so, trusting God without conditions isn't easy.

Just ask Shadrach, Meshach, and Abednego, three devout Jewish men living in the pagan land of Babylon (Daniel 3). To secure the loyalty of his subjects, King Nebuchadnezzar made a massive golden idol, approximately ninety feet high and nine feet wide. Then he hosted a dedication celebration with all the leaders throughout the Babylonian Empire, including Shadrach, Meshach, and Abednego, with the following requirement: "Whoever does not fall down and worship will immediately be thrown into a blazing furnace" (v. 6).

When the king discovered that Shadrach, Meshach, and Abednego would not bow down to the idol as ordered, he was "furious with rage" (v. 13). Bystanders thought Nebuchadnezzar's ultimatum would be the men's undoing. Quite the contrary. They knew where their loyalty lay before they were ever put to the test.

"King Nebuchadnezzar, we do not need to defend ourselves before you in this matter. If we are thrown into the blazing furnace, the God we serve is able to deliver us from it, and he will deliver us from Your Majesty's hand. But even if he does not, we want you to know, Your Majesty, that we will not serve your gods or worship the image of gold you have set up" (vv. 16–18).

I've always found this section of text fascinating. On the one hand, they claim absolute belief that God will deliver them: "He *will* deliver us" (v. 17, emphasis mine). Then in the next breath, they seem to recant: "But even *if he does not*" (v. 18, emphasis mine). Is this proof of their lack of faith? Are they questioning God's power or will? Or are they creating a plan B just in case God doesn't come through? Been there, done that.

I don't think so. Their confidence wasn't in their agenda. Their confidence was in a Person. So whether God delivered or didn't deliver, they remained steadfast in their belief because their salvation was sure, even if they turned to ash.

As pastor Tim Keller said in a sermon, "They were spiritually fireproof long before they were physically fireproof."[35]

John 6 paints this tension with definitive strokes. When the crowds caught up with Jesus and the disciples in Capernaum, they asked him plainly, "What must we do to do the works God requires?" (John 6:28). Rather than give them a long list of to-dos and to-don'ts, Jesus pointed to the one thing they found the most difficult: "The work of God is this: to believe in the one he has sent" (v. 29). He then went on to call himself the Bread of Life (vv. 35, 48) and challenged his hearers to "eat" his flesh and "drink" his blood (vv. 48–58). They recoiled, thinking he spoke of cannibalism. But Jesus was talking not about literal bread and physical sustenance but eternal life.

What God wants most from us isn't our good works or our well-intentioned efforts. What He wants from us is the one thing we struggle most to give: our trust.

"On hearing [Jesus' teaching], many of his disciples said, 'This is a hard teaching. Who can accept it?' . . . From this time many of his disciples turned back and no longer followed him" (vv. 60, 66).

Too many times I've watched as men and women who once claimed Jesus as Lord turn back and no longer follow Him. Perplexed by Jesus' words and people who poorly represent Him, they choose a life without faith and faith's questions rather than a life that makes room for both.

It isn't always easy to trust a God you don't always understand. It isn't easy to trust His love when your ongoing suffering makes it appear as if He's anything but real or good. The longer our questions linger without satisfactory answers, our confusion grows and our confidence wanes. After all, some marriages thrive while others fail. Some children come home while others remain at a distance. And some diagnoses end in healing while others end in death. Who decides those who get their miracle and those who, to their deep grief, don't?

Who can explain to me the seemingly mercurial nature of this world held in the hands of an impossible to understand God?

"'You do not want to leave too, do you?' Jesus asked the Twelve. Simon Peter answered him, 'Lord, to whom shall we go? You have the words of eternal life. We have come to believe and to know that you are the Holy One of God'" (vv. 67–69).

Ah, exactly. To whom else shall I go?

My God is able to deliver me, and He will deliver. But even if He does not . . .

I trust you, God. I trust you.

Five-Minute Faith Builder

All these people were still living by faith when they died. They did not receive the things promised; they only saw them and welcomed them from a distance.

—HEBREWS 11:13

Make a list of all the situations and people that are causing you to lose sleep. Maybe it's a child who isn't making the decisions you'd have them make, a job that is feeling less and less like the right fit, an outstanding bill you have no idea how you're ever going to pay, unresolved questions about Christianity that leave you wondering whether you're believing in the wrong thing. Whatever is troubling you, write it down in the margins here or in your journal. Then write Peter's words to Jesus in John 6:68: "Lord, to whom shall we go? You have the words of eternal life." If you're able, add these words of your own: "I trust you, God. I trust you."

$$\boxed{\text{DAY 5}}$$

ABSOLUTE SURRENDER

*God does not ask you to give the perfect surrender in
your strength, or by the power of your will; God is
willing to work it in you. . . . And that is what we should
seek for—to go on our faces before God, until our
hearts learn to believe that the everlasting God Himself
will come in to turn out what is wrong, to conquer
what is evil, and to work what is well-pleasing in
His blessed sight. God himself will work it in you.*
—ANDREW MURRAY, *HUMILITY AND ABSOLUTE SURRENDER*

It took a third cancer diagnosis to force me to let go of my life.
Not that I had much choice in the matter, but for the year
before, I'd been tirelessly attempting to control my fate. I changed
my diet, eating less sugar and more cruciferous vegetables. I ran daily,
finally completing my second half-marathon. At the counsel of a medical doctor who also specialized in alternative medicine, I started a
strict regimen of supplements, as well as yoga, breathing exercises,
consistent rest, and stress mitigation. I did everything I could possibly
do to be a strong, healthy forty-three-year-old woman who wanted to
outsmart cancer.

In the middle of that herculean effort, I received my third cancer diagnosis. Nine months after the second.

Defeated doesn't capture my grief. I'd wielded all the weapons within my reach. Nothing worked. No matter how hard I gripped the steering wheel of my life, cancer reminded me, with painful clarity, that I have far less control than I think I do.

The truth of this terrified me.

But it also set me free.

As terrifying as a cancer diagnosis can be (and it is), it is equally as terrifying if not more so to feel the full responsibility of all your life's outcomes. If everything is within our control and we are the gods of our own lives, then who are we to blame when our children make choices we don't want them to? Or when a marriage crumbles before it even gets a fair start? Or when a job ends, a church fails, a relationship disintegrates, or a diagnosis comes? We can either look inward and take all the blame on ourselves, or we can look around us and grow bitter at all the ways life and people have let us down. Either way, we will end up gripping our lives so tightly that we'll squeeze the life right out of them.

On the night of Jesus' arrest in the garden, Peter remained convinced he had enough courage to endure whatever was about to happen.

- "Lord, I am ready to go with you to prison and to death" (Luke 22:33).
- "But Peter insisted emphatically, 'Even if I have to die with you, I will never disown you'" (Mark 14:31).
- Hours later, when soldiers came, Peter grabbed his sword, weapon ready to follow through on his promise. "Then Simon Peter, who had a sword, drew it and struck the high priest's servant, cutting off his right ear" (John 18:10).

Peter's passion and intention were noble, at least in part. At some level, he was indeed ready to defend Jesus. But he wasn't yet ready to surrender to Him. And that is what Jesus wanted him to do, to allow God's redemption plan to unfold: "'Put your sword back in its place,' Jesus said to him, 'for all who draw the sword will die by the sword. Do you think I cannot call on my Father, and he will at once put at my disposal more than twelve legions of angels? But how then would the Scriptures be fulfilled that say it must happen in this way?'" (Matt. 26:52–54).

Don't miss what Jesus is saying here, because it's important.

Peter was willing to follow Jesus as long as following looked like what he wanted it to: a sword and a physical battle. But God's plan was bigger than a midnight arrest in a garden. And when following Jesus meant surrendering, he found it easier to run than to relinquish (v. 56). To be clear, this is not a commentary on war versus passivism or even a commentary on traditional versus alternative medicine.

It's about surrender.

Absolute surrender means following Jesus when He calls you to pick up your weapons or when He tells you to lay them down, to fight the battle or withdraw from it, to go where He's sending you or stay where He's put you. It involves surrendering your need to understand along with your need to control, relinquishing both the outcomes and the means to the God who is writing a story bigger than the small one you're living. And then trusting Him to bring new life even at the cost of death.

Not easy, I know. Good heavens, *I know*.

Ultimately, we will surrender to something. Whether we surrender to ourselves, our relationships, our work ethic, or our team of doctors, we will place our trust in whatever we believe has the power to steer our course the right direction. But surrender to the wrong source, and you'll find your life even more out of control. Everything has an expiration date. Our bodies wear out, our relationships change, children grow up, and careers take a turn. Sooner or later, it all comes to an end.

Except for God Himself. Surrender to Him and you'll always be in good hands.

Five-Minute Faith Builder

Whoever wants to be my disciple must deny themselves and take up their cross daily and follow me. For whoever wants to save their life will lose it, but whoever loses their life for me will save it. What good is it for someone to gain the whole world, and yet lose or forfeit their very self?

—LUKE 9:23–25

Surrender often requires more effort than sword fighting, especially for those of us who have made it our life's work to stay in absolute control. Surrender feels risky, dangerous, unmooring. What if it doesn't work out? What if letting go is the first step toward our downfall?

Or what if the opposite is true?

Consider what is holding you back from absolute surrender. How's that working out for you? What would it take for you to relinquish control?

PART 5

THE PRACTICE OF CONTENTMENT

When the apostle Paul wrote a letter of mentorship to a young Timothy, he offered the following advice: "But godliness with contentment is great gain" (1 Tim. 6:6). When you read Paul's words before and after these, it seems Timothy had encountered some Jesus followers who aimed to leverage their status as Christians for a financial profit. Paul wanted him to understand that success isn't measured in money or titles but in a heart of contentment, an essential practice for an enduring faith.

Contentment doesn't come easy to those of us raised in the shadow of the American dream. We've been conditioned to believe that what we have is not enough. We want more. The gospel, though, proposes a better way. Contentment is a greater wealth than all the money in the world. And when we discover its riches for ourselves, we'll find the losses a bit easier to release.

THE TRAP OF ENTITLEMENT

The life of faith is lived one day at a time, and it has to be lived—not always looked forward to as though the "real" living were around the next corner. It is today for which we are responsible. God still owns tomorrow.
—ELISABETH ELLIOT

Teaching my kids to pray has been more challenging than I thought. We pray as a family twice a day: at the dinner table, and at bedtime. We pray at other times, of course. But at a minimum, this amounts to fourteen times per week or 728 times per year. But even with all that prayer practice, God help us, we still haven't nailed the landing.

My youngest prays the same script every night at a speed that would likely beat Usain Bolt in the hundred-yard dash. The prayer is finished before my upper eyelids hit the lower, and I'm pretty sure it could blow-dry my hair.

And then there is my second son. He's now nearly thirty years old, but when he was still a preteen living in our home, he'd turned his prayer into a CliffsNotes variety: "Dear God, thank you for the three Fs. Amen."

Boom, done.

What are the three Fs, you ask? Friends, food, and family. And there you have it. He did, in fact, cover the bases.

Somewhere along the way, in our desire to teach our children solid faith practices, we failed to help them understand the meaning and purpose behind the practices. Spiritual disciplines are not check boxes that, when checked with religious predictability, guarantee equally predictable results. Instead, spiritual disciplines help us build spiritual muscles that enable us to more consistently walk out daily life in connection with God. They are the means to the end, not the end. God is who we're aiming for.

Which brings us to the practice of contentment. Contentment turns transactional, check-box prayers into conduits of relationship. Often our prayers are little more than a shopping list. Like a spiritual Instacart, we identify everything we need, and expect God to do our shopping and then show up on our doorstep between 5:00 and 6:00 p.m., bags in hand. If He's late or (gasp!) is missing items, we leave a less than glamorous review and maybe ding His tip. Celestial customer service is severely lacking.

This approach to prayer smells of the rot of entitlement. It's one thing to ask God for what we want and need. It's another to base our affection for and trust in Him on His impeccable delivery.

The first and necessary ingredient to contentment is a solid acceptance of the fact that we are entitled to nothing.

(Go ahead and read that again.)

God doesn't owe us. We don't deserve a big house, a happy marriage, well-behaved children (or children at all), a six-figure income, and a long and healthy life including a peaceful death in our sleep. The American dream isn't something you and I are entitled to, whether or not we are American. It's okay to desire those things, even to work toward them. But like worms in fruit, entitlement only spoils our desires before we take the first bite out of them.

Consider this list: Running water. Indoor toilets. Access to medical care. The physical ability to work. The ability to hear, see, taste, touch, feel. Clean water in which to wash dishes, clothes, our bodies. First responders who show up when we call 911. Public (and safe) places of worship. Education. Clean air. A seventy-eight-year life span. Tylenol. The internet. The ability to read and write.

Chances are that today you took at least one of these things for granted. But millions of other individuals didn't have your same luxury. You drank a glass of water without fearing it would make you sick. You attended church without fear of being arrested. In the course of this single day, you will breathe approximately twenty-two thousand times without thought. And probably like most of us, you will breathe clean air. When these daily provisions are commonplace, we not only lose the wonder of them but grow to believe we're entitled to them.

In his book *The Rest of God*, author Mark Buchanan says it this way:

Thankfulness is a secret passageway into a room you can't find any other way. It is the wardrobe into Narnia. It allows us to discover the rest of God—those dimensions of God's world, God's presence, God's character that are hidden, always, from the thankless. Ingratitude is an eye disease every bit as much as a heart disease. It sees only flaws, scars, scarcity. Likewise, the god of the thankless is wary, stingy, grudging, bumbling, nitpicky. . . . But to give thanks, to render it as Scripture tells us we ought—in all circumstances, for all things, to the glory of God—such thanksgiving becomes a declaration of God's sovereign goodness. Even more, it trains us in a growing awareness of that sovereign goodness. You cannot practice thankfulness on a biblical scale without it altering the way you see.[36]

Is the rot of entitlement spoiling your contentment? Have you slipped into the bad habit of making demands and complaints? Habits can be broken, and new habits developed. Determine to shift the way you think and speak away from entitlement toward gratefulness. Not only will it make the people around you happier, you'll feel more peace and contentment than ever before.

Five-Minute Faith Builder

Do everything without complaining and arguing, so that no one can criticize you. Live clean, innocent lives as children of God, shining like bright lights in a world full of crooked and perverse people.

—PHILIPPIANS 2:14–15 NLT

Recently, Doug Miller, a Colorado pastor, delivered a sermon on complaining. In it, he reminded us of two important facts about an ungrateful spirit.

First, it offends God. It devalues all that God has already done for us (Ex. 14:11–12; 16:2–3; Num. 11:1–2).

And second, it has consequences. In the case of the Israelites, God grew tired of the grumbling, and the complainers never made it to the promised land (Num. 14:27–28, 30).

Miller then presented the solution to an entitled and ungrateful heart, as seen in 1 Thess. 5:16–18 (NLT): "Always be joyful. Never stop praying. Be thankful in all circumstances, for this is God's will for you who belong to Christ Jesus." It's a 1-2-3 approach:

1. Always be joyful. Catch yourself when you're not.
2. Never stop praying.
3. Give thanks in all circumstances.

Spend five minutes considering God's extraordinary generosity toward you. Set a timer and list the many ways you've experienced His generosity today. Yes, just today. When the timer goes off, review your list. Then pray this simple prayer:

You've given me far more than I deserve, Father. You are good, full of generous grace and love. I receive these things with gratitude and contentment. Thank you!

$$\boxed{\text{DAY 2}}$$

DO NOT FORGET

*I think we delight to praise what we enjoy because the
praise not merely expresses but completes the enjoyment; it is
its appointed consummation. It is not out of compliment
that lovers keep on telling one another how beautiful
they are; the delight is incomplete until it is expressed.*
—C. S. LEWIS, *REFLECTIONS ON THE PSALMS*

I hate this family! You never do anything for me!"
Her voice ricocheted off the family room walls, white hot with
fury. Although my husband sat only a few feet away, she'd aimed her
words at me. My heart. It hurt, which is what she'd intended.

Those of you who have raised teenagers have likely experienced a
similar moment (or twelve) in your parenting adventure. More times
than not, it comes on the heels of some type of discipline or perceived
injustice. A phone taken away, a party invitation denied, a privilege
revoked. In the heat of disappointment and frustration, the easiest person to accuse is the one who caused the pain—in this case, me. So she
pulled out the big guns and let me have it.

"All I've ever wanted is a mom who loved me! But you can't do
that, can you?!"

Aaaaaand there it is. The coup de grace. The final shot, and her mission complete.

Everything in me wanted to retaliate with all the evidence to the contrary. The countless sacrifices and struggles, the long thankless days of loving and supporting, teaching and comforting. Parenting was no picnic, and yet I kept showing up, forgiving, praying, asking for forgiveness, and trying again. And yet in a moment of disappointment, she tossed years of love's evidence into the trash.

I wanted to retaliate. At times I have, God forgive me. But this time, I took a breath and asked a single question: "Don't you remember how you crawled into my lap and we cuddled under the blanket this morning?"

Only a few hours before, she'd come into the family room needing reassurance. Putting my book to the side, I pulled her to me and held her with one arm while my other hand played with her hair. We didn't say much of anything; we didn't need to. She needed to be held and loved. I did both.

With that reminder, her anger cooled. She still wasn't happy, but the memory was enough for her to reconsider her perspective. Feelings, though valid, don't always reflect reality.

As much as I'd like to blame this whole situation on adolescent hormones (which played a part, no doubt), I don't have enough fingers and toes for all the times I've done the same to God, and I'm well past adolescence. Nothing causes spiritual amnesia quite like suffering. The more disappointment I feel today, the less I remember God's deliverance yesterday.

This is why God reminded the Israelites over and over again to be careful not to forget.

- "Only be careful, and watch yourselves closely so that you do not forget the things your eyes have seen or let them fade from your heart as long as you live" (Deut. 4:9).

- "Be careful that you do not forget the LORD, who brought you out of Egypt, out of the land of slavery" (6:12).
- "When you have eaten and are satisfied, praise the LORD your God for the good land he has given you. Be careful that you do not forget the LORD your God, failing to observe his commands, his laws and his decrees that I am giving you this day" (8:10–11).
- "Remember that you were slaves in Egypt and the LORD your God redeemed you from there" (24:18).

In contrast, the books of Judges and Psalms expose glimpses of the Israelites' poor memory:

- "No sooner had Gideon died than the Israelites again prostituted themselves to the Baals. They set up Baal-Berith as their god and did not remember the LORD their God, who had rescued them from the hands of all their enemies on every side" (Judg. 8:33–34).
- "How often they rebelled against him in the wilderness and grieved him in the wasteland! Again and again they put God to the test; they vexed the Holy One of Israel. They did not remember his power—the day he redeemed them from the oppressor, the day he displayed his signs in Egypt, his wonders in the region of Zoan" (Ps. 78:40–43).
- "When our ancestors were in Egypt, they gave no thought to your miracles; they did not remember your many kindnesses, and they rebelled by the sea, the Red Sea" (Ps. 106:7).

This is only a sample of the Scriptures that talk about the importance of remembering. In the face of pain, we are prone to forget. God's proven faithfulness today fades into doubt tomorrow. My book *Relentless* attempts to counteract this tendency to forget, by searching for and memorializing God's faithfulness in altar stones, visible evidences of God's relentless nearness, not just for today's challenge but for all of the challenges on tap for tomorrow.

In the parable of the sower, Jesus talks about the danger of this kind of forgetfulness. A farmer plants seed in the hope of a harvest. But only a small portion of seed takes root and grows. Take note of what Jesus says happens to the seed that falls on the rocky ground or among the thorns: "The seed falling on rocky ground refers to someone who hears the word and at once receives it with joy. But since they have no root, they last only a short time. When trouble or persecution comes because of the word, they quickly fall away. The seed falling among the thorns refers to someone who hears the word, but the worries of this life and the deceitfulness of wealth choke the word, making it unfruitful" (Matt. 13:20–22).

Remembering God's faithfulness is the rich soil your faith needs to thrive when your world falls apart. It doesn't mean today's circumstances will be easy or pain free. But the same good God who delivered you before will deliver you again. His record is solid, His character true. Remember this. And be at rest.

Five-Minute Faith Builder

Return to your rest, my soul,
for the LORD has been good to you.

—PSALM 116:7

In Psalm 116:7–9, the psalmist gives us a trusted practice for finding peace in difficult circumstances: "Return to your rest, my soul, for the LORD has been good to you. For you, LORD, have delivered me from death, my eyes from tears, my feet from stumbling, that I may walk before the LORD in the land of the living." The author charges us to *remember* God's faithfulness in previous seasons, to recall the various ways He has delivered us from our physical suffering ("delivered me from death"), our emotional suffering ("my eyes from tears"), and our experiential suffering ("my feet from stumbling"). For today's Faith Builder practice, create a three-column list using these three categories. Then ask God to remind you of the ways He has delivered you in the days before this one. Return to your rest, friend, for the Lord has been good to you.

DAY 3

A GRATEFUL LIFE

Faith is an expression of the fact that we exist so that the infinite God can dwell in us and work through us for the well-being of the whole creation. If faith denies anything, it denies that we are tiny, self-obsessed specks of matter who are reaching for the stars but remain hopelessly nailed to the earth stuck in our own self-absorption. Faith is the first part of the bridge from self-centeredness to generosity.

—MIROSLAV VOLF

Few things ruin a rousing pity party like meeting someone who has it harder than you do. For example, I once spent a weekend with a woman with eight children. Yes, *eight*. And immediately all my go-to conversation starters about being a mom of six became irrelevant, like complaining of a paper cut to someone who has lost an arm. *What?! Only six children?! A cake walk, sister.* Let's just say that, while we were together, I kept my complaints of exhaustion and exorbitant grocery prices to myself.

Gratitude is a powerful tool for making peace with an imperfect life. Pain makes us myopic. Like blinders on a horse, suffering shrinks the scope of our vision until all we can see are the most difficult parts of our reality. We cease to see any good in the middle of the bad. That doesn't mean we don't have reason to shout or pout at the size of the grocery bill. But gratitude works like vision-correcting glasses. It brings back into focus the possibilities pain had blurred. And this gives us new strength and hope through the struggle.

One of the few stories that appears in all four gospel accounts—Matthew, Mark, Luke, and John—is the story of Jesus feeding the five thousand. Mark sets up the miracle this way: "Taking the five loaves and the two fish and looking up to heaven, he gave thanks and broke the loaves" (Mark 6:41).

There are at least two important insights in this verse. First, Jesus looked up. The Greek word here means "to look up, to receive sight."[37] In a sense, Jesus looked up to get clarity. He needed to see things from God's point of view.

Then with clear vision aimed the right direction, He gave thanks. The word here is *eulogeo*, from *eu* (good, well) and *logos* (word). Together, it means "to bless, speak well of. To praise, commend . . . to consecrate with thanksgiving." It's the word from which we get *eulogy*, a speech or piece of writing that praises someone or something highly, typically someone who has just died.[38]

We think of eulogies as something reserved for funerals. But we can eulogize someone while they're still living, and it can be even more meaningful. Years ago, I attended a celebration of life for someone with a terminal illness. Rather than wait for his death, we celebrated his life while he was still with us. It remains an impactful experience for me.

In this story, Jesus eulogized His Father *before* He fed the five thousand. In His hands He held five small loaves of bread and two small fish. It wasn't enough to feed the twelve disciples, let alone a crowd of thousands. Jesus practiced gratitude anyway. When the stakes were high and the human need great, Jesus chose to give thanks while everyone was still hungry. He gave the eulogy *before* the miracle happened.

Why? Because the goodness of the Father doesn't depend on the giving of the gift.

Each evening, after I've finished preparing dinner and before our youngest three children are allowed to dive in and satisfy their hunger, we circle the table, holding each other's hands, while one of us gives thanks. In part, we're teaching our children to daily acknowledge God's goodness before our stomachs are full. It's an attempt to help them understand that gratitude is less a response to a gift and more a way of approaching the Giver. It's an attitude more than an action.

If you're unsure where you land on the gratitude scale, think back on the last time you didn't get something you wanted. A job, an opportunity, a gift, a spouse, a child, a recognition, a parking place. What is your typical response to a disappointment? That might be a clear indicator of your gratitude attitude. By the way, if you're feeling your toes a bit bruised, have no fear: mine are downright bloody. Because if there is one thing I don't handle well, it's disappointment.

If I feel I've earned it or am owed it, I've turned my relationship with God into nothing more than a transaction. And yet Jesus is setting the example here, as He looks up toward heaven and chooses to eulogize God while giving thanks for the too-small meal: *All of this is yours, Father. It's already yours. Thank you. You're a good Father.*

With praise on His lips, the food was multiplied to feed thousands that day, with basketfuls of leftovers.

Entitlement delivers a hunger that cannot be satisfied.

Gratitude satisfies the hunger of not only the one who serves the meal but everyone who pulls up a patch of green grass and shares in the supper.

"They all ate and were satisfied" (Mark 6:42).

Yes, that. And twelve basketfuls of leftovers besides.

Five-Minute Faith Builder

Remember this: Whoever sows sparingly will also reap sparingly, and whoever sows generously will also reap generously. Each of you should give what you have decided in your heart to give, not reluctantly or under compulsion, for God loves a cheerful giver. And God is able to bless you abundantly, so that in all things at all times, having all that you need, you will abound in every good work.

—2 Corinthians 9:6–8

Read these words again: "Pain makes us myopic. Like blinders on a horse, suffering shrinks the scope of our vision until all we can see are the most difficult parts of our reality." How have you seen this truth play out in your struggles? When has a challenge caused a bit of nearsightedness, making it difficult for you to see beyond your pain? As you reflect, try to stay in a place of compassion and not judgment. Then consider: How might gratitude deliver clearer eyesight and new strength? These are tough questions. Don't be afraid to linger with them for a few moments, even if you don't yet have clear answers. Then close with this prayer:

Father, your goodness doesn't depend on your giving me the gift I desire. I still ask you for your healing, deliverance, answer, and provision. But regardless of what you do or don't do, I choose to believe that you are good. And that you love me.

THE FLIP SIDE OF GENEROSITY

*Just as words lose their power when they are
not born out of silence, so open loses its meaning
when there is no ability to be closed.*
—Henry J. M. Nouwen

I love texting. Don't expect me to call. I'd rather tear off my toenails. But I text better than a teenager. Even so, texting can be a bit of a minefield if expectations are involved. Which is why my favorite kind of text goes something like this: "Hey! Been thinking of you. We're overdue for a coffee date. No rush, I know you have your hands full. Just know I'd love to connect if/when you have a minute. You're loved!"

I have a couple of friends who send me similar texts, and every time they do, something settles deep in my soul. Why? Because they are generous on love and stingy on expectations. And that's the sweetest kind of gift, because it's full of grace.

When it comes to generosity, we typically think of money. But generosity is more than financial. It involves not only the tangible but also the intangible, not only what we give away but also what we keep to ourselves.

For example, generosity includes giving forgiveness, patience, understanding, kindness, encouragement, time, and skills. And it also looks like withholding criticism, condemnation, sarcasm, hasty judgments, and contempt, to name a few. Although financial generosity can deliver relief, is there anything more reassuring than receiving forgiveness or patience when you're downright desperate for it?

What I have discovered in my fifty-some years of living and giving is that my ability to be generous with others—in both material and nonmaterial ways—is directly connected to my internal sense of contentment, no matter my circumstances. When contentment is lacking and I'm feeling desperate and anxious, I tend to frontload any generosity with expectation of a return. I'm like a bank account gone dry, looking for deposits wherever I can find them. But when I choose to anchor myself to God's ready forgiveness and love and settle deep into the contentment of His generosity, I give from the abundance of what I already have without expectation of any kind of return. There, the wounds I experience at the hands of others heal much more quickly. I'm able to withhold judgment and criticism, and I sleep more soundly at night and experience a new freedom in the morning. When I allow my family members, friends, neighbors, coworkers, and even strangers around me to be their in-progress selves without resentment or rejection, I find a little more acceptance of myself too.

When I choose to be generous with what I give as well as with what I withhold, a different kind of calm settles, regardless of my reality. As Proverbs 11:25 says, "A generous person will prosper; whoever refreshes others will be refreshed."

It's not easy, I know. As I write, I feel convicted about a few grudges I've been nursing. This flip side of generosity feels costly. At times, it's easier to write a check than to forgive an emotional debt.

But God understands this too. God's generosity with us does not come without cost. We often forget this, assuming that the abundance of God's love and forgiveness means it costs Him nothing to give them away. Dr. Tony Evans said it this way: "Forgiveness is not pretending like it didn't happen or it didn't hurt. That's lying. Forgiveness is the decision to release a debt regardless of how you feel."[39] And that is what God has done for us.

- "When Jesus landed and saw a large crowd, he had compassion on them, because they were like sheep without a shepherd. So he began teaching them many things" (Mark 6:34).
- "But God demonstrates his own love for us in this: While we were still sinners, Christ died for us" (Rom. 5:8).
- "He saved us, not because of righteous things we had done, but because of his mercy. He saved us through the washing of rebirth and renewal by the Holy Spirit, whom he poured out on us generously through Jesus Christ our Savior" (Titus 3:5–6).
- "If any of you lacks wisdom, you should ask God, who gives generously to all without finding fault, and it will be given to you" (James 1:5).

God's generosity with us is unparalleled, both in what He gives (compassion, healing, time, forgiveness, the Holy Spirit, beauty, wisdom) and in what He withholds (rejection, condemnation, separation, isolation). May we, having received more than what we could have asked for or imagined, offer a similar generosity in return.

Five-Minute Faith Builder

The one who has knowledge uses words with restraint,
and whoever has understanding is even-tempered.
Even fools are thought wise if they keep silent,
and discerning if they hold their tongues.

—PROVERBS 17:27–28

Read this sentence again: "Generosity includes giving forgiveness, patience, understanding, kindness, encouragement, time, and skills. And it also looks like withholding criticism, condemnation, sarcasm, hasty judgments, and contempt, to name a few." Circle the acts of generosity on this list that are most meaningful to you. What else would you add to the list? Now consider your own generosity. Which of these come easily to you, and which are more difficult? Think of one way you can be generous with someone else today. Spend a few moments confessing your struggle with generosity, and ask Jesus to help you pay the price to live a more generous life.

$$\boxed{\text{DAY 5}}$$

ENOUGH

Go back, then, a little way to the choice mercies
of yesterday, and though all may be dark now,
light up the lamps of the past, they shall glitter
through the darkness, and thou shalt trust in the Lord
till the day break and the shadows flee away.
—CHARLES SPURGEON, *MORNING AND EVENING*

I fell in love with the mountains at fourteen years old. For most of my childhood, I lived in central Illinois, surrounded by soybean and corn fields. My only experience of elevation occurred on Sundays when the choir sang four-part harmony right out of the hymnal and a soprano belted out the final high note with gusto.

Although my family lived in California and Arizona for my first seven years, with their own version of mountainscapes, I didn't grasp the magnitude of a full mountain range until a family road trip at fourteen. Over the span of two weeks, we took in the Rocky Mountains, Jackson Hole and the Grand Tetons, the Badlands, and Mount Rushmore and the Black Hills. Like different children of the same parents, each stop came with similar and yet entirely unique beauty. I was smitten.

Two weeks later, I knew our trip neared its end when miles of flat soybean fields once again filled my vision. And although it was beautiful in its own way (yes, I miss that view at times), I ached to go back to the mountains, and I hoped that someday, somehow, I'd find a way to return.

Sometimes the answers to our prayers don't look like we expect them to.

I ended up moving to Colorado on another road trip at the age of twenty-six, while my seven-month-old son cut four teeth in his car seat behind me. A few weeks before, my then-husband lost his job and took a new one in the Rocky Mountain State. Without going into detail, it was a painful move, filled with enormous losses that were outside my control. Although my car was pointed toward the mountains, my heart was broken at what I'd left behind.

For my first year in Colorado, I struggled with significant grief and depression, buried by too many injustices and unsure how to walk through them to life on the other side. Although the mountains sat outside my window, I couldn't see them through the fog of my grief. Then a little more than one year later, the final nail of grief was hammered into place when I watched my husband's car drive away for the last time. I was twenty-seven years old with a twenty-two-month-old son, alone in a city with no family and few friends.

When I think back on that season, I ache for that young woman. She felt consumed by her losses, angry and bitter at life's inequity, resentful of her innocent hope in happy endings. I see her disappointment in people and her disillusionment in faith. She had every reason to feel that way.

But that's not all I see. I also see provision.

Somewhere in the middle of all that darkness, light broke through. I still remember the day. Only a handful of months had passed since I'd become a divorced, single young mother. Caught up in the never-ending cycle of full-time work and caring for a toddler, I had little time for anything else. Even so, I knew enough to consistently get outside and exercise. And on this particular day, I'd strapped my baby boy into our jogging stroller and set off for a run through the neighborhood. About halfway, I stopped. It was an extraordinarily beautiful day, the Colorado sky vibrant blue, the sunlight filtering through the clouds, the trees a lush green. I looked to the west and took in the wide expanse of the Colorado Rocky Mountains. That was the moment it occurred to me: *Out of all the places I could live when my world fell apart, I'm glad it was here.*

Then I closed my eyes and let the sun warm my face. For the first time in too long, I felt hope bloom. *How good of you to bring me here, God. Thank you. I don't know why you allowed all of this pain and loss. But thank you for bringing me here while I walk it out.*

Over the months and years before, all my dreams of a good life—marriage, family, ministry—had been crushed. There was no salvaging what had been. I could only grieve what I'd once hoped for and make peace with what was. Even so, God had seen fit to bring me to Colorado before the bottom fell out. I felt His nearness, His tenderness, in the mountains. And so, in kindness, God brought me to the one place where I could still get glimpses of Him even when everything safe and familiar was gone.

Divine provision in a place of extraordinary pain. He does it every time, if we stop long enough to look.

I've now lived in Colorado for more than twenty-five years. In that time, I've walked through a slew of additional challenges. Although they were painful, each time I faced another impossible mountain, I found myself taking another look at the ones outside my front door.

How good of you to bring me here, Father.

And whether hiking a lonely trail or simply taking in the view from my front yard, I know where my help comes from: "I lift up my eyes to the mountains—where does my help come from? My help comes from the LORD, the Maker of heaven and earth" (Ps. 121:1–2).

Divine provision. It is enough.

Five-Minute Faith Builder

I lift up my eyes to the mountains—
    where does my help come from?
My help comes from the LORD,
    the Maker of heaven and earth.

He will not let your foot slip—
    he who watches over you will not slumber;
indeed, he who watches over Israel
    will neither slumber nor sleep.

The LORD watches over you—
    the LORD is your shade at your right hand;
the sun will not harm you by day,
    nor the moon by night.

The LORD will keep you from all harm—
    he will watch over your life;
The LORD will watch over your coming and going
    both now and forevermore.

—PSALM 121

If you struggle to see God's provision in your pain, you're not the only one. Pain—whether physical, emotional, or spiritual—is consuming. It demands your attention, blinding you to everything else. This is your body doing what it was made to do, and it's good. But to allow pain to become your sole focus will rob you of the hope of what's possible on the other side. Today, look for evidence of God's provision exactly where you are. Then read Psalm 121 aloud as a prayer. Ask Him to show you His kindness, right here. Write down whatever comes to mind, and then give thanks. You don't have to be happy about your broken heart, but you can be grateful that He's tending to it as only He can.

$$\boxed{\textbf{PART 6}}$$

THE PRACTICE
OF SHALOM

Shortly before He was arrested and crucified, Jesus told the disciples (and all of us) about the gift He longed to give us in our grief: "I have told you all this so that you may have peace in me. Here on earth you will have many trials and sorrows. But take heart, because I have overcome the world" (John 16:33 NLT). Oh, how we long for peace! And Jesus says we can have it, but perhaps not in the way we imagine.

When we think of peace, we often think of the absence of struggle and conflict, pain and loss. We want life to be smooth, predictable and expected. But Jesus' peace—the shalom of heaven—delivers calm in relationships rife with conflict, serenity in seasons of struggle, and His presence in places of pain. He is the eye in the middle of the storm. And when we hide ourselves in Him, we discover a peace that is far more securing than a perfect life.

$$\boxed{\text{DAY 1}}$$

TO BE WHOLE

*As a child may cry out in pain even when sheltered
in its mother's arms, so a Christian may sometimes
know what it is to suffer even in the conscious presence
of God. . . . But all will be well. In a world like
this, tears have their therapeutic effects. The healing
balm distilled from the garments of the enfolding
Presence cures our ills before they become fatal.
The knowledge that we are never alone calms the
troubled sea of our lives and speaks peace to our souls.*
—A. W. TOZER, THE KNOWLEDGE OF THE HOLY

You're famous," my daughter announced while I prepped dinner for the family.

I rolled my eyes while chopping something decidedly less than glamorous.

"Hardly," I scoffed.

She continued to state her case, my other children joining in, talking about Google searches and social-media followers and all the other evidence that today's youth equate with celebrity status.

I just shook my head and continued chopping, a bit more contemplative than before. Although I've written a few books, I'm anything but famous. I've never seen my face on the cover of a grocery-store magazine, never been on the *Today Show*, never walked a red carpet or received an invitation to the White House. But to kids who grew up under the influence of YouTube and TikTok, celebrity status is the ultimate aim. And to them, the fact that a few videos show up in a Google search means I'm famous, even if the spotlight is the last thing I want.

For the next several minutes, I did my best to sober their perception, to explain the dark side of celebrity culture, especially in Christian spheres of influence, the downfall of that much attention, and the danger that is idolizing anyone or anything that isn't God Himself. But like attempting to row a canoe upstream with toothpicks, I did little to alter their culture-driven aspirations. After all, society promises only what the human heart craves: significance.

But like anything counterfeit, attention cannot deliver significance any more than Monopoly money can buy a new car.

We weren't made to be famous. We were made to be whole.

Our drive for attention is, at its core, a desire to validate our existence. We need to know we matter, that there is something about us that is worthy. We want to stand out, to be one of a kind, and then to know without any doubt that we were created with purpose and, as a result, we belong.

Celebrity culture fools us into thinking that this kind of worth can be found with photographs and followers, video hits and social-media likes. But it is never enough. The person with a hundred followers dreams of a thousand, and the person with ten thousand video views aspires to have ten million. We're so hungry for the attention that comes with the spotlight that we'll post compromising pictures, controversial threads, and irreverent humor hoping the algorithms will deliver what we crave.

We think we need a spotlight. But that only leaves us exposed.

What we really need is shalom. And that can be found only in the light of God's presence.

In the Old Testament, *shalom* is a Hebrew word that is often translated as "peace." But shalom is more than a temporary state of peacefulness. According to Leslie Allen, senior professor of Old Testament at Fuller Theological Seminary, shalom means wholeness or completeness. "An important extended meaning is 'peace,' which is also the meaning people generally attribute to the word. But the cognate adjective, *shalem*, is used of whole, uncut stones used for building an altar in Joshua 8:31. . . . A *shalem* heart refers to an undivided attitude of wholeheartedness."[40] We need more than the temporary peace we feel after watching a satisfying movie or waking up from a refreshing nap. We need an enduring wholeness that roots us right where we are, whether we're standing in a spotlight of adorers or sitting alone in the dark without a single friend.

We need more than a feeling. We need a filling.

In Jewish tradition, *shalom* is a blessing often used in greetings and farewells. It wishes the other person the peace that comes from wholeness with God and with others. Although *shalom* doesn't appear in the Greek New Testament, the word *eirene* (pronounced eye-RAY-nay) is often believed to be the New Testament equivalent. Similarly translated as "peace," *eirene* means "tranquility, repose, calm; harmony." *The Hebrew-Greek Key Word Study Bible* says it this way:

"Such a state of peace is the object of divine promise and is brought about by God's mercy, granting deliverance and freedom from all the distresses that are experienced as a result of sin. Hence the message of salvation is called the gospel of peace (see Acts 10:36 and Eph. 6:15), for this peace can only be the result of reconciliation with God."[41]

Shalom (or *eirene*) is the completeness that comes from an abiding awareness of our rightness with God. Then as an offshoot of individual shalom, we strive to live shalom with others. Jamie Arpin-Ricci, in his book *Vulnerable Faith*, describes it this way: "Shalom is what love looks like in the flesh. The embodiment of love in the context of a broken creation, shalom is a hint at what was, what should be, and what will one day be again. Where sin disintegrates and isolates, shalom brings together and restores. Where fear and shame throw up walls and put on masks, shalom breaks down barriers and frees us from the pretense of our false selves."[42]

When we practice shalom, we stop aching for cotton-candy attention and instead experience God's never-ending affection. Only in God's light are we fully seen, fully known, *and* fully loved. Then, safe in His shalom, we turn around and offer the same to others.

Famous doesn't deliver. Wholeness does.

The kind of wholeness that comes only from God's shalom.

Five-Minute Faith Builder

How lovely is your dwelling place,
    LORD Almighty!
My soul yearns, even faints,
    for the courts of the LORD;
my heart and my flesh cry out
    for the living God.
Even the sparrow has found a home,
    and the swallow a nest for herself,
    where she may have her young—
a place near your altar,
    LORD Almighty, my King and my God.
Blessed are those who dwell in your house;
    they are ever praising you. . . .
Better is one day in your courts
    than a thousand elsewhere.

—PSALM 84:1–4, 10

God's light couldn't be more different than the spotlight. Whereas fame's spotlight exposes you to inspection, criticism, and shame, God's light opens you to intimacy, healing, and security. The first light leaves you vulnerable and empty; the second light makes you strong and full. Even better, dwelling in God's presence doesn't require a platform or a crowd. It isn't a place you drive to or a special room in which you sit. You can dwell in God's presence in the waiting room of a doctor's office as easily as in the backwoods of a national forest. Today spend five minutes sitting in the light of God's presence. Say these words out loud:

Father, with you I am seen. I am safe. And I am loved. Fill me with your light. And make my heart crave you more than all else. Amen.

$$\boxed{\text{DAY 2}}$$

THE RESPITE OF SOLITUDE

*In solitude, God begins to free us from our
bondage to human expectations, for there we
experience God as our ultimate reality.*
—RUTH HALEY BARTON

On a hot pink, three-by-five index card in my Bible is a single word, four letters in caps: PRAY.

I use it as a bookmark, marking my daily reading spot as I work through the books of the New Testament. Each day, it points me to where I need to begin my reading. But it also reminds me of the one spiritual discipline I am most likely to neglect.

Getting alone to pray isn't easy for me. Although I regularly communicate with God and try to listen for His voice in the busyness of each day, I do a poor job of making space for uninterrupted, unhurried prayer. Each morning as I sit in what I call my prayer chair, I'm like a two-year-old trying to sit still in church. I squirm, attempting to wrestle my thoughts into some kind of mature order. It goes something like this:

"Father, thank you for another beautiful day of life. I love you, and I am so grateful for you. I'm fully aware that I deserve nothing from your hand, and yet you've given me everything I need and more besides."

That reminds me, I need to get milk when I head into town later today. Oh! And the bank. I need to go to the bank.

Did I pay the kids' field-trip fees yet? I think that was due today. Ugh, I hope I didn't forget. I should probably check my email. Good thing my phone is right here.

Fifteen minutes later, after being sucked into the black hole that is my phone: *Where was I? PRAYING. I was praying.* "God, you are good. Holy, righteous, and yet full of mercy."

The library books on my shelf catch my eye.

Those books were due last week. I probably owe a small mortgage in overdue fees again. Why can't I remember?! For the love—Jesus, take the wheel. Where was I?

You get the idea. My attempts at time alone with God are feeble at best. And yet I keep returning to try again for one reason: I know I need it. Without this anchor of solitude with God, I am sunk. He is "my refuge and my fortress, my God, in whom I trust" (Ps. 91:2). Outside of these frazzled moments of solitude with God lie a host of people and problems that never seem to end. Real life is complicated and chaotic. So I retreat to a quiet place to pray. To listen. To just sit and *be* with Him And although I fail at it miserably, I will keep practicing. Because in solitude with Him I find shalom.

When Jesus faced the final hours before His arrest, prosecution, and death, He too felt the tension of living in a broken world. So He retreated to the garden of Gethsemane, accompanied by a few of those closest to Him, to pray.

"Then he said to them, 'My soul is overwhelmed with sorrow to the point of death. Stay here and keep watch with me'" (Matt. 26:38).

Leaving His friends behind, He found a place of solitude and poured out His heart to the Father, asking for relief and peace.

Later, when Jesus caught His friends sleeping, He again challenged them: "'Couldn't you men keep watch with me for one hour?' he asked Peter. 'Watch and pray so that you will not fall into temptation'"

(vv. 40–41). In the moment of Jesus' great agony, He gave those closest to Him three instructions: Stay. Watch. And pray.

The Greek word for "keep watch" is a word that is used three times in Matthew 26, emphasizing its importance. It's the word *gregoreuo*, which means "to watch, refrain from sleep . . . a mindfulness of threatening dangers which, with conscious earnestness and an alert mind, keeps one from all drowsiness and all slackening in the energy of faith and conduct."[43] In view of His pending arrest and death, Jesus urged them to stay mindful of what was at stake: their faith!

Jesus wasn't asking something of them that He didn't do Himself. The gospel writer Luke says that Jesus "often withdrew to lonely places and prayed" (Luke 5:16). He needed a strength that could come only from alone time with God, the kind that wouldn't be muted by the conversations and chaos that come when constantly surrounded by others. Life is serious business, and death sits closer than we think. "The spirit is willing, but the flesh is weak," Jesus reminded them (Matt. 26:41). That'll preach. I feel those nine words every time I promise myself I won't have ice cream before bed ever again. One thousand amens.

Stay, watch, and pray, Jesus urged them. That night, Peter didn't. Years later, though, Peter finally understood Jesus' warning on that dark night so long ago, because he turned around and offered a similar challenge to us: "Be alert and of sober mind. Your enemy the devil prowls around like a roaring lion looking for someone to devour. Resist him, standing firm in the faith, because you know that the family of believers throughout the world is undergoing the same kind of sufferings" (1 Peter 5:8–9).

Like me, Peter needed solitude, that place where we finally see clearly the war we're waging and the God who has the weapons we need to fight it.

We have good intentions, but low follow-through. The weight of the world makes our eyes heavy, and it's easier to slip into sleep even while we're awake. As a result, our shalom is sometimes spotty.

But as Catholic priest Henri Nouwen remarked, "Prayer is not a pious decoration of life but the breath of human existence."[44] The one in the garden waits for us still, ready and willing to breathe life into our places of death. Will you sit with Him, even if your solitude looks a bit like a squirmy toddler? Time alone with Him is better than no time at all. And the more we keep watch with Him, the more we learn how to pray like Him, pouring our hearts out to the Father. And ready to persevere when the dark comes.

Five-Minute Faith Builder

But Jesus often withdrew to lonely places and prayed.

—LUKE 5:16

Find a quiet place to be alone. It can be outside or inside, morning, afternoon, or evening, at home or away from home. Time and location don't matter as much as the spirit in which you enter. For five minutes, sit in solitude, without break or interruption. (You might need to let family members and roommates know what you're doing so they don't panic and call 911.) Once you've settled in, take a few slow, deep breaths, in and out. Then with eyes closed, picture yourself sitting with Jesus in the garden. Stay. Watch. And pray.

```
DAY 3
```

MADE FOR SABBATH REST

The root idea of Sabbath is simple as rain falling, basic as breathing. It's that all living things—and many nonliving things too—thrive only by an ample measure of stillness. A bird flying, never nesting, is soon plummeting.
—MARK BUCHANAN, THE REST OF GOD

I love to work, always have. At eleven years old, I started babysitting evenings, weekends, and summers. By the time I turned sixteen, though, I wanted a job that didn't involve diapers and temper tantrums. Turns out kids are a handful. So I applied for an open position at a little Christian gift store in our local mall, a place called (wait for it) . . . The Love Shop.

Yes, my first W-2 employment experience sounded a smidge like an adult entertainment operation. Trust me when I say I was the object of giggles and grins from my peers as a result. Even so, it was a great first job. The best, in fact. Owned by a lovely Christian family, they treated me like one of their own and gave me more responsibility than I deserved. They trusted me, and as a result I matured, developed budding leadership skills, and discovered a deep love of work.

This love continued into my late teens and twenties, when I worked in the pediatric and medical-surgical departments of two hospitals, with the American Heart Association, in corporate America, and eventually building multiple successful businesses of my own.

By 2020, I once again returned to corporate employment as an executive, right when a global pandemic changed the way we work and relate to one another. I loved my job—the challenge, the growth, the relationships, the new skills.

One of the most valuable lessons I learned in that season came when author John Eldredge spoke to a group of our business clients about how to live more wholly, even as the world fractured. Although months have passed since that day and I've forgotten most of what John said, he made one statement I won't forget. I wrote it down on a Post-it Note and put it on my computer to make sure of it: "This is where I labor, but this is not where I live."

John reminded me that my work and career, as much as I may enjoy them, are not the sum of my life. They are only a small part. Just as God's work of creation required a sabbath rest, my life and work require the same.

For months after I heard John say those words, I started my workday with a glance at that yellow Post-it Note. Although too many meetings and endless responsibilities filled my calendar, I began the day with a reminder that my life does not consist of my work. Work is important, yes. Bills need to be paid, groceries purchased, and a family provided for. And it is okay to enjoy my job. But I can't love work to the neglect of rest. That's a formula for a fast demise. The only way I could keep doing what I loved was to love rest—and the rest of my life—too.

In spite of his power and wealth, King David understood the tension between work and rest. He was good at his job as king. He was a mighty warrior, a strong leader, a passionate visionary. He was made for kingship. And yet he understood that his role was only one slice of his life. He needed to find the source of his strength elsewhere: "Truly my soul finds rest in God; my salvation comes from him. Truly he is my rock and my salvation; he is my fortress, I will never be shaken" (Ps. 62:1–2).

This is where I labor, but this is not where I live.

Centuries later, Jesus said something similar: "Come to me, all you who are weary and burdened, and I will give you rest. Take my yoke upon you and learn from me, for I am gentle and humble in heart, and you will find rest for your souls. For my yoke is easy and my burden is light" (Matt. 11:28–30).

A yoke is a work tool, and this is a work metaphor. When we read these verses, it's tempting to think of this Christianity thing as just another place where we labor. That's why many fall out of love with faith. It's a job that wears us out, a rigorous work we have no competence to complete.

But we're thinking of it all wrong. Jesus is saying, in so many words, that we will undoubtedly yoke ourselves to something in the hope that it might finally deliver peace and rest. Family, careers, financial stability, relationships, ministry, status, skills, and talents. There seems to be no end to the places where we try to find ourselves. Even religion.

But Jesus isn't asking us to yoke ourselves to any of those things. He's asking us—urging us—to yoke ourselves to a relationship.

To Himself.

He's asking us to learn *from* Him, not merely *about* Him. Then, whether we are working, cooking, vacationing, fighting, exercising, playing, grieving—whatever it is we are doing at any particular moment—we are yoked with Him in it. And that means, in spite of the struggle, we can be at rest.

He is our center, our resting place. No matter where we are.

Five-Minute Faith Builder

In peace [shalom] I will lie down and sleep,
for you alone, LORD,
make me dwell in safety.

—PSALM 4:8

Watchman Nee, leader of an indigenous Christian movement in the 1930s in China, said, "For Christianity begins not with a big DO, but with a big DONE. . . . There is no limit to the grace God is willing to bestow upon us. He will give us everything, but we can receive none of it except as we rest in him."[45] For today's Faith Builder exercise, move away from all distractions (cell phone, I see you) and create a mini-Sabbath, right here, regardless of what day it is. Then once you have stilled and quieted your mind and soul, read Psalm 23 slowly. Let the words ground you. You live with the Shepherd. He is your home. Hear the quiet waters, feel the refreshing of your soul. And rest.

The LORD is my shepherd, I lack nothing.
    He makes me lie down in green pastures,
he leads me beside quiet waters,
    he refreshes my soul.
He guides me along the right paths
    for his name's sake.
Even though I walk
    through the darkest valley,
I will fear no evil,
    for you are with me;

your rod and your staff,
    they comfort me.

You prepare a table before me
    in the presence of my enemies.
You anoint my head with oil;
    my cup overflows.
Surely your goodness and love will follow me
    all the days of my life,
and I will dwell in the house of the LORD
    forever.

—PSALM 23

$$\boxed{\text{DAY 4}}$$

PEACE IN PLACES
OF FEAR

It was one of those moments when I thought the Lord had left me. I turned away and said, "God?" And immediately He spoke to me. . . . He said, "My, child, did I not say to you that when you pass through the waters, and these are waters of sorrow, that I would be with you? And through the floods, they would not overflow you? And neither will the fire kindle upon you?" I said, "Alright, Lord." In the night hours the tears would flow, and then my Lord would come to me and He would speak peace to my heart, and I learned experimentally about the comfort of the Holy Spirit.

—DARLENE DEIBLER ROSE, *EVIDENCE NOT SEEN*

My friend Kathleen sent me a picture of a snake today. A close-up. And when I say close-up, I mean close enough to see him chew his dinner.

Hello, shudder response. I'm glad you still work.

One of her dogs found it in their yard, just a ten-minute walk from my house.

Her question to me via text: "Bull snake? Or rattlesnake?"

My response: "Either way, eeew."

Living in the country means we have our share of critters. Mice. Lizards. Bats. Squirrels. And yes, snakes. Plenty of snakes. Including bull snakes and rattlesnakes. Rattlesnakes are territorial and poisonous. Deadly. Bull snakes can bite but are harmless. We don't mind the bull snakes (as long as they mind their own business) because they keep the mice and other rodents in check. Even better, it turns out they also like eggs for breakfast—rattlesnake eggs.

The tricky thing is that bull snakes look very similar to rattlesnakes. Worse, bull snakes are masters at mimicking the rattlesnake in an effort to protect themselves. What they lack in poison they make up for in acting skills. Impressive, unless the snake is five feet away and you can't tell the difference.

The trick is to master the ability to tell the difference from a distance. For example, bull snakes are darker and often more brown, and rattlesnakes more yellow, with a diamond pattern on their backs. Rattlesnakes have a thinner neck and triangular head, whereas the bull snake has a thicker neck and flat head. And then, of course, the rattlesnake has the telltale rattle at the end of its tail, and the bull snake doesn't.

Look closely (not too close) and you'll know when you should be afraid. The only alternative is to be afraid all the time and avoid going outside for fear of encountering something that can kill you. And when you live in the country, that isn't any way to really live.

I've battled fear in different seasons of my life. As a child, I feared sleeping in the dark, falling off my bike, getting in trouble, failing a test, not having a boyfriend. As an adult, my fears changed but were no less intimidating. I was afraid of not being good enough, of making too many parenting mistakes, of being rejected or abandoned, of losing a job or losing my kids. I feared not having enough money, enough faith, enough time.

Fear isn't fun. I know because for twelve years of my life I've lived with cancer and the fact that it can come back. At times, I found myself chronically looking over my shoulder, waiting for the next strike that would poison my happy life. But fear wears a soul out, and I grew tired of it.

At times, we have good reason to be afraid. The human brain is wired to warn us when we face danger, which is a good thing because the human experience is full of danger.

But it's one thing to be alert to danger, another thing to be hyper-vigilant to it. We must learn how to listen to the alarm bells but then master the ability to distinguish between those things that hold the power to destroy a life, and those things which only hold the power to inconvenience it.

Jesus said it this way: "Do not be afraid of those who kill the body but cannot kill the soul. Rather, be afraid of the One who can destroy both soul and body in hell. Are not two sparrows sold for a penny? Yet not one of them will fall to the ground outside your Father's care. And even the very hairs of your head are all numbered. So don't be afraid; you are worth more than many sparrows" (Matt. 10:28–31).

To practice shalom is to live immersed in the truth of God's love and grace, the only antidote to life's poisonous strikes. While we may not understand our suffering, we are not alone in it. And we can be confident that nothing we experience will be wasted when we remain in His able hands.

In God's words to His people, "'Though the mountains be shaken and the hills be removed, yet my unfailing love for you will not be shaken nor my covenant of peace [shalom] be removed,' says the LORD, who has compassion on you" (Isa. 54:10).

Do not fear, my friend. The Prince of Shalom has come. And He will walk you through.

Five-Minute Faith Builder

Peace I leave with you; my peace I give you. I do not give to you as the world gives. Do not let your hearts be troubled and do not be afraid.

—JOHN 14:27

What do you most fear? Is it a relationship? A job? An unpaid bill or unresolved medical condition? Being human is hard, and it seems to get harder the older we get. A lot can go wrong. Make a short list of your greatest fears in the margin or in your journal, and then take a moment to consider each one. How can practicing shalom deliver more peace? How can God's total love and unflinching faithfulness make you whole, even while so much of your life remains unresolved? Then personalize the following verses from Psalm 46 into a prayer as one small way to practice shalom today. In parentheses, I've included my own personalization to help you get started.

> God is (you are) our (my) refuge and strength,
>   an ever-present help in trouble (walking through
>   health challenges and mothering my children).
> Therefore we (I) will not fear, though the earth give way
>   and the mountains fall into the heart of the sea,
> though its waters roar and foam
>   and the mountains quake with their surging (though
>   so much feels out of my control and I don't know
>   how things will end up).

There is a river whose streams make glad the city of God,
the holy place where the Most High dwells.
God is (you are) within her (me), she (I) will not fall;
God (you) will help her (me) at break of day.

—PSALM 46:1–5

DAY 5

TO LIVE SHALOM

The true measure of our character is how we
treat the poor, the disfavored, the accused,
the incarcerated, and the condemned.
—BRYAN STEVENSON, *JUST MERCY*

I gripped the three-by-five index card in my left hand as the hum of the radiation machine kicked in. Bolted to the table beneath me and with a mask over my head, I could not move. The claustrophobic circumstance caused my heart to race and skin to sweat for the long minutes I lay confined. My saving grace? The three-by-five card in my left hand with a single name I'd penned on it an hour before.

For six weeks, five days per week, I underwent external beam radiation on my head and neck after my third diagnosis of squamous cell carcinoma of the tongue. Radiation is never an enjoyable experience, regardless of the type or body part. But when you start shooting radiation at the head, the fallout is significant. By the end of six weeks, I had extensive burns from my nose down to my shoulders, inside and out. My throat was swollen, my vocal cords were burned, the risk of choking was constant. It took multiple attempts to complete my final sessions because of my inability to breathe and swallow while reclining.

For every one of those six weeks of days, I held a three-by-five index card in my left hand with a new name written on it each day. Each represented someone who suffered. The sources were different, their stories varied. But for six weeks, their pain became my own. And while radiation beams beat up my body, I prayed for the name in my left hand until the day's treatment was done.

I can no longer remember when I decided to do this or the impetus behind it. I'm keen to credit God's wisdom rather than my own. All I know is that, years later, I believe it is the reason I look back on those brutal weeks with more peace than trauma. While interceding for others, I discovered a measure of peace for myself.

Part of individual shalom is tied up in the shalom of others, making it a communal experience, in whatever communities we find ourselves. As the cross reconciled to God a world in conflict, when we carry on God's work of shalom, it is, likewise, a work of reconciliation, even if it means taking up a cross to do so.

Jer Swigart, a church planter, professor, and cofounder of the Global Immersion Project, found his definition of peace and shalom radically altered when his mentor told him to start his shalom practice by looking at the cross. "Peace, then, as defined by the cross, is the restoration of all things. It is the holistic repair of severed relationships, the mending of the jagged divides that keep us from relationship with one another. According to Colossians 1, the implications of the cross were comprehensive and conclusive: God had waged a decisive peace in Jesus, and it had worked. That meant that God is the Great Peacemaker and restoration is the mission of God."[46]

In his letter to the Colossians, Paul likewise spoke of the cross as the inspiration for our living shalom: "For God was pleased to have all his fullness dwell in him, and through him to reconcile to himself all things, whether things on earth or things in heaven, by making peace [shalom] through his blood, shed on the cross" (Col. 1:19–20).

Jesus, the embodiment of God's presence with humankind, left the shalom of heaven to enter into the conflict of humanity, denying His own comfort to make it possible for you and me to be comforted. Because Jesus embodied shalom, we can't escape His call for us to do the same. We mustn't hole up in our peace-filled corners, content to retreat and reflect and let the problems plaguing our nation and world fall on someone else's agenda. We are reflections of God's presence, ambassadors of the gospel of good news. Swigart continues, "While God's peace was decisively waged in Jesus, God's peace becomes real in the world when we embrace our vocation as everyday peacemakers. . . . Our physical presence and practice in sync with the Spirit of the Resurrected One cause us to become the ongoing embodiment of God's restorative mission—his shalom—here and now."[47]

But how do we embody shalom right here, for ourselves and for our world? It begins, I believe, by not allowing any individual peace to blind us to the lack of peace around us. We must push ourselves to see and acknowledge suffering and injustice. To ask questions, to listen, to advocate. Whether it is the marginalization of individuals or groups, social or racial inequities, or simply the mistreatment of those who are different from us, as shalom bearers we stand on the front lines, meeting needs and demonstrating Christ's love.

In his book *Just Mercy*, Bryan Stevenson steps all over my comfortable toes: "We are all implicated when we allow other people to be mistreated. An absence of compassion can corrupt the decency of a community, a state, a nation. Fear and anger can make us vindictive and abusive, unjust and unfair, until we all suffer from the absence of mercy and we condemn ourselves as much as we victimize others."[48] When we neglect shalom around us, we neglect shalom within us, to our detriment.

But the opposite is also true. When we work for shalom for others—in our homes, neighborhoods, communities, nations, world—we find ourselves shoulder to shoulder with the one whom the prophet Isaiah spoke of:

The Spirit of the Sovereign Lord is on me,
>> because the Lord has anointed me
>> to proclaim good news to the poor.
He has sent me to bind up the brokenhearted,
>> to proclaim freedom for the captives
>> and release from darkness for the prisoners,
to proclaim the year of the Lord's favor
>> and the day of vengeance of our God,
to comfort all who mourn,
>> and provide for those who grieve in Zion—
to bestow on them a crown of beauty
>> instead of ashes,
the oil of joy
>> instead of mourning,
and a garment of praise
>> instead of a spirit of despair.
They will be called oaks of righteousness,
>> a planting of the Lord
>> for the display of his splendor.

—ISAIAH 61:1–3

Five-Minute Faith Builder

But the wisdom that comes from heaven is first of all pure; then peace-loving, considerate, submissive, full of mercy and good fruit, impartial and sincere. Peacemakers who sow in peace reap a harvest of righteousness.

—JAMES 3:17–18

One at a time, take stock of your home, neighborhood, church, school, workplace, city, state, nation, and the world. On a scale of 1 to 10, how would you rate shalom in each? What evidence supports your rating? Consider those people and places that most need peace. Brainstorm some ways you can be a conduit of shalom in your circles of influence this week. Then assign yourself a due date for taking the first step to implement these ideas. Remember, your shalom—my shalom—is tied in part to others' shalom.

PART 7

THE PRACTICE OF FORGIVENESS

Is anything costlier than forgiveness? When disappointed or disregarded, betrayed or rejected in a relationship, to forgive the wrong feels as painful as the wound itself, to wipe the slate clean as impossible as healing. And yet to live with unforgiveness is to live with a corrosive and more lethal cancer, one that eats away at our peace and faith until we have little of either left. The road to faith in a God who will right all wrongs and redeem all regrets is paved with the never-ending work of forgiveness. That means if we want to have a faith that will not fail, even though our world and relationships may, we must choose the kind of forgiveness we've been given, over and over again, no matter the cost.

$$\boxed{\text{DAY 1}}$$

THE CHARGES AGAINST GOD

*Our anger does not surprise or fluster Him. He knows
all about it. It was God's rage that nailed the Son of
God to the cross. He gets anger. He wrote the book
on it. And He invites people, people like you and me,
to come and air our grievances and complaints to Him.
And the good news is you can do so without weakening
your faith. You can do so and be all the better for it.*

—JONI ERICKSON TADA,
FOREWORD TO *CRY OF THE SOUL*

Sometimes I get angry with God.

Not just a little miffed but red-faced angry.

This may come as a shock to you, especially if you have long
believed big feelings are sinful. That's okay. I once believed the same.
And yet here we are. We can sit prim and proper in church, hands
folded and smiles plastered on our faces, but whether we admit it or
not, these human bodies come with feelings. Sometimes big feelings,
and rightly so. I've come to believe that God is far less appalled at my
big feelings than I am.

So yes, I get angry with God. For example, I think of two friends who have long wanted a house full of children. They have a strong extended family, solid community network, financial stability, a beautiful home. But no matter how many times they try to have children, whether by birth or adoption, it ends in disappointment. Then I consider another family, wrought by addiction, dysfunction, and abuse, and they can't seem to stop having babies. I don't understand the injustice of it.

God, why won't you do something?

I think of one of the most powerful leaders in the world terrorizing his own citizens while recruiting the wealthy to be his lackeys. Buffered by his ego and absent of conscience, he spreads terror at home and abroad, exacting vengeance on whoever he wants, whenever he wants. As he rises in power, seemingly unfettered, so does my anger.

God, when will you put an end to evil and defend the poor?

My friends of color share stories I thought happened only in history. I was wrong. So I listen to the names they've been called in the fast-food drive-up window, the epithets screamed from open car windows while their brown son plays in the front yard, the extra measures they must take while browsing at a department store or driving on a highway to avoid any hint of suspicion. It makes me angry, and I want to rage.

God, why do you tolerate the injustice?

And then, of course, I consider my own story. For most of my childhood I prayed for a family that loved Jesus and served Him in full-time ministry. Instead, I have a Humpty Dumpty, broken-and-glued-back-together family of children and adults who are hanging on by a thread, and a failing body to boot. I keep praying for relief, and yet my troubles keep piling on.

God, I've followed you my whole life. Why won't you do something? Haven't I endured enough?

At times it's easier to stay tucked away in anger than to air my grievances to God. Anger works as a shield, a safer emotion than grief or confusion. So we hide behind our rage, safely ensconced in our anger and refusing to face a hard reality: God is God and we are not.

This is what Job experienced when he gave voice to his grief and made his complaint to God. God answered, and His answer wasn't easy to hear. (If you have the stomach for it, see Job 38–41.) After a stretch of unexplained and unrelenting suffering, Job voices his complaint. And in these final chapters of Job, God responds. You will not find platitudes, cliches, or reassurances. God says nothing at all about Job's suffering or the reason for his pain.

Instead, through four chapters of pointed facts and rhetorical questions, God reminds Job of who He is. Although Job never abandoned his faith, his perspective had become obscured by his pain. All he could see was what he'd lost. And he'd lost a lot.

But God knew Job needed more than soft cliches. He needed a powerful God. He needed a God of absolute authority and supremacy. He needed to know, in no uncertain terms, that although it appeared life was running off the rails, the God he'd loved and trusted his entire life was far more terrifying than he could imagine and was still in absolute control. His presence is permanent. His power undisputed. His wisdom incomparable. His authority immutable.

So God reminded him. In a speech that will make your toes curl. And although Job's losses remained, his comfort finally came. Not through the resolution of circumstances but through a reminder of place and position. Don't believe me? Read these words and hear the hints of comfort in his voice: "Then Job replied to the Lord: 'I know that you can do all things; no purpose of yours can be thwarted. You asked, "Who is this that obscures my plans without knowledge?" Surely I spoke of things I did not understand, things too wonderful for me to know. You said, "Listen now, and I will speak; I will question you, and you shall answer me." My ears had heard of you but now my eyes have seen you. Therefore I despise myself and repent in dust and ashes'" (Job 42:1–6).

Although I've yet to receive satisfactory answers to my hardest questions, I can now say like Job, "My ears had heard of you but now my eyes have seen you." I have seen God. And although I still feel anger, I also find new comfort every time I see God on His throne, regardless of what He has or has not done. I see Him, in His glory and majesty and authority and holiness, and in response I can do little more than fall on my face. I still cry out to Him. But I also worship Him.

"Who then is able to stand against me? Who has a claim against me that I must pay? Everything under heaven belongs to me" (Job 41:10–11).

Indeed.

Five-Minute Faith Builder

Why, Lord, do you stand far off?
Why do you hide yourself in times of trouble?
—PSALM 10:1

Have you ever felt angry at God? Are you angry right now? Take your complaint directly to Him. Don't allow yourself to hide behind your anger but tell Him the truth about it. Trust me, He already knows. And then allow Him to reorient your perspective a little bit. Yes, He aches with you, weeps with you, mourns with you. But He has not abdicated His throne. He is still very much in charge, and He wants you to see Him seated squarely there. Not because He's on a power trip but because He knows a glimpse of His authority will finally deliver security. If and when you're ready, pray Job's prayer in Job 42:1–6 for yourself. May your ears hear and your eyes see the God who loves you and is with you.

$$\boxed{\textbf{DAY 2}}$$

THE CHARGES AGAINST ME

Poor and proud we all are. We will not, if we can help it, take our seat in the lowest room, though that is our proper place. Grace alone can bring us to see ourselves in the glass of truth. To have nothing is natural to us, but to confess that we have nothing is more than we will come to until the Holy Spirit has wrought self-abasement in us.

—CHARLES SPURGEON, "THE HAPPY BEGGAR"

The story appeared in various news outlets yesterday: Another megachurch pastor accused of inappropriate behavior with a member of his church. Flirty text messages, drunken nights spent in a hotel room, purportedly confirmed by investigation and evidence. They say it is only the beginning. What yet lurks in the history of his forty-year ministry?

Over the past several years, I've experienced a growing disappointment in many Christian leaders. Although there remain an honorable and faithful few, the list of leaders and pastors I long admired grows smaller and at a rapid pace. These are the men and women I've listened to and learned from. They've been my counselors and teachers in the internet age, allowing me access to fresh voices outside my geography. Their mentorship, even virtually, impacted the trajectory of my faith.

In some cases, my trust was misplaced.

Of course, the pedestal-toppling has happened in less public places too, only a few miles from my front door. Affairs, sexual abuse, financial impropriety, cover-ups, and split-inducing conflicts. When I think of the many churches I've been connected to in my fifty years of life, I could fill too many pages with the sordid details and resulting disillusionment, much to my deep grief. Why do these things continue to happen? Why do those who claim to love Jesus most appear to follow Him the least? Shouldn't faith leaders be held to a higher standard? Shouldn't they know better?

Yes. Churches and ministries must learn from our mistakes and establish rigorous accountability, a commitment to integrity, and consequences when needed. We cannot allow evil to be done in the name of ministry or convince ourselves that a cover-up preserves the gospel. Shame on us.

As much as I'm angered by the confirmed abuses of Christian leaders, I am relieved that my faults are far less public. I'm confident that if a team of investigators dug through my every word, action, and thought, they would uncover enough dirt to fill several volumes. Criticisms, judgments, and gossip. Harsh words and retaliations.

My character, in spite of my good intentions, wouldn't survive an investigation. The evidence would stack up, becoming a mountain of accusation I'd have no ability to refute. It wouldn't take a jury long to conclude that my character doesn't always live up to my claims.

When I place myself under the glaring light of divine righteousness and submit to the scrutiny of the one to whom I'm accountable, the sin I see shames me. I am selfish, unforgiving, compromising, ungrateful, rebellious, evil. As Paul penned in Romans 7:15, "I do not understand what I do. For what I want to do I do not do, but what I hate I do."

That I've not yet committed the wrongs the world deems more grievous is not a result of my being better or righteous. Quite the opposite. I am equally capable of misdeeds, given the right circumstances and choices.

"So I find this law at work: Although I want to do good, evil is right there with me. For in my inner being I delight in God's law; but I see another law at work in me, waging war against the law of my mind and making me a prisoner of the law of sin at work within me. What a wretched man I am! Who will rescue me from this body that is subject to death?" (vv. 21–24).

This is the question we must all ask. Who will rescue me? Who will save me from myself? Who will look at the investigative report and determine that, in spite of the overwhelming evidence, I am worth rescue?

"Thanks be to God, who delivers me through Jesus Christ our Lord!" (v. 25).

Leaders—Christian and otherwise—will rise and fall as long as humans walk the earth. They can't escape their wretched humanity any more than you and I can. Yes, some need to suffer the consequences of their choices, legal and otherwise. That too is part of it. But you and I mustn't forget that the evidence against us is just as damning. We don't deserve God's mercy any more than those who fall farthest from their pedestals.

But thanks be to God! When we confess sin in the light of Truth and accept the charges against us, Jesus offers grace and forgiveness. Unmerited, undeserved.

That's the only platform strong enough on which to stand, no matter who rises and who falls.

Five-Minute Faith Builder

If you, LORD, kept a record of sins,
Lord, who could stand?
But with you there is forgiveness,
so that we can, with reverence, serve you.

—PSALM 130:3–4

Take a moment to consider your spiritual record. Consider the words you said, the thoughts you entertained, the actions you took. Consider the criticisms and unforgiveness you've nurtured like a garden filled with weeds that you water and feed, to the detriment of the grasses and flowers you could have grown instead. Then read Psalm 130 out loud as a personal prayer, using your name in place of "Israel." Stand in the light of His righteousness, acknowledging the charges against you. The price is paid. You are redeemed.

Out of the depths I cry to you, LORD;
    Lord, hear my voice.
Let your ears be attentive
    to my cry for mercy.

If you, LORD, kept a record of sins,
    Lord, who could stand?
But with you there is forgiveness,
    so that we can, with reverence, serve you.

I wait for the LORD, my whole being waits,
    and in his word I put my hope.

I wait for the LORD
     more than watchmen wait for the morning,
     more than watchmen wait for the morning.

Israel, put your hope in the LORD,
     for with the LORD is unfailing love
     and with him is full redemption.
He himself will redeem Israel
     from all their sins.

—PSALM 130

$$\boxed{\text{DAY 3}}$$

THE COST OF FORGIVENESS

The greatest human act is forgiveness.

—HENRI NOUWEN, *YOU ARE THE BELOVED*

I woke up early this morning rehearsing an old wound again.

One a.m. and I'd already turned that thing around and around in my mind like a two-carat diamond. Only it wasn't nearly as lovely.

I kept playing back the events before, during, and after, dissecting each word and nuance, each inflection and neglect, trying to unravel the thing until I could understand it or somehow go back and change it. As if doing what I'd already done dozens of times before would somehow yield a different result.

Instead, I felt hurt all over again, as if the thing had happened moments before, not months or years before. Why did I keep picking at the sore, making it raw once again? Why did I let it cost me sleep?

I'm confident I'm not the only one who plays this middle-of-the-night game. It's a game of horrible odds, promising zero winners and infinite losers. And yet play it we do, over and over again, at the price of our peace. No matter how hard I try, I can't seem to let it go. I am human, after all.

That's the point, isn't it? I am human, as are the people I do life

THE PRACTICE OF FORGIVENESS

with, including my tired husband and grouchy teenagers. As is the woman who nearly barreled over me with her shopping cart and the driver who screeched past me with a harsh blare of his horn. And yes, as is the one who cost me my sleep last night.

Humans, every one. Prone to sass and snap, bark and bite.

Like me, they grow weary and worn down. They feel overwhelmed by the ongoing slog through a difficult life. They carry traumas and experience inconveniences every day, many of which I can relate to but know nothing about. Are they not allowed forgiveness too?

As it turns out, I want to guzzle grace, but I don't want to give it. I want a full cup of God's mercies, ready to quench my thirst for affection even when I'm difficult to love. And yet, at times, I remain reluctant to offer the tiniest drop of mercy to those who likewise thirst for it.

In his book *You Are the Beloved*, Henri Nouwen claims, "The greatest human act is forgiveness: 'Forgive us our sins, as we forgive those who have sinned against us.' Forgiveness stands in the center of God's love for us and also in the center of our love for each other. Loving one another means forgiving one another over and over again."[49] We buy flowers and gifts, pay for dinners and destinations all in an effort to buoy our relationships with evidence of our love. But forgiveness? We often refuse to cover the cost, even when it is what our relationships need most of all. And when those we love wound us again and again, the price of forgiveness goes up with each infraction, exacting a price they'll never be able to pay.

Grappling with the parameters of forgiveness, Peter asked Jesus a pointed question: "Lord, how many times shall I forgive my brother or sister who sins against me? Up to seven times?" (Matt. 18:21). Forgiveness has a price cap, right? Surely God doesn't expect us to forgive on repeat. That would be naive, foolish. Forgiveness must have limits. Peter thought seven sounded generous.

Rather than answer Peter's question directly, Jesus tells a story about a servant in significant debt. The servant was buried by bills he couldn't pay—an amount Matthew describes as ten thousand bags of gold—and the master planned to throw the servant in jail until he could repay the full debt, an amount he couldn't pay back in several lifetimes. No one accrues that much debt without a long history of horrible decisions. Enough is enough.

Desperate for mercy, the servant begged another chance and promised to pay back every cent he owed, yet another promise he wouldn't keep. The master, moved by his plea, did even more than the servant asked, more than he deserved. He set the man free and cleared his debt, at his own cost. The servant left a free man.

But the servant's freedom went only as far as his pocketbook. As he left, he came across a man who owed him one hundred silver coins, pocket change compared with his own debt. Rather than offer mercy, he choked the man and threw him in jail, unmoved by his cries. Mercy received failed to become mercy given. When the master found out, he had the servant thrown back in jail. As a result, the servant ended up even more in debt than before (Matt. 18:21–35).

Before hearing this story, Peter had asked about the limits of forgiveness. He wanted a black-and-white scorecard, some way to ensure the cost didn't get out of control.

Jesus threw the scorecard out.

"This is how my heavenly Father will treat each of you unless you forgive your brother or sister from your heart" (v. 35).

Unforgiveness costs only the person nursing it. And it's a cost that comes with compounding interest. Yesterday's unforgiveness turns into tomorrow's bitterness, and yesterday's distance turns into tomorrow's loneliness. The longer you and I refuse forgiveness, the greater the debt we carry, until we are all alone and cannot carry it at all.

Besides, forgiveness isn't about how much the other person owes. It's about how much of your debt has already been paid.

How much forgiveness do you want from your Father? A mercy that runs out? Or a mercy that runs free? If you and I want to live unbound by the debts that continue to accumulate against us, the only remedy is to offer the same mercy in return.

Forgiveness is costly, no doubt about it. But it's the only way to live debt free.

Five-Minute Faith Builder

Blessed are the merciful,
for they will be shown mercy.
—MATTHEW 5:7

Forgiveness always comes at a cost. We can either demand the person who wronged us pay the debt, or we can pay that debt ourselves by forgiving it. Either way, it costs something. Unforgiveness imprisons us emotionally as we nurse the wound. Forgiving someone who wronged us also inflicts pain. I feel the wound, but I choose to bear it and ultimately end up free. When Jesus asks us to forgive, He's fully aware of the cost. Forgiveness cost Him physically, mentally, emotionally, spiritually. The wound went deep, to death. He chose to bear it anyway. For today's Five-Minute Faith Builder, spend time practicing forgiveness for those who have wronged you. At a later time, you may need to go directly to the person. For now, spend time with Jesus by speaking forgiveness over those who have let you down. In the spirit of the Lord's Prayer, pray, "Forgive me my debts, as I forgive those who have debts against me" (Matt. 6:12).

DAY 4

THE PEACE OF FORGIVENESS

The power of just mercy is that it belongs to the
undeserving. It's when mercy is least expected that
it's most potent—strong enough to break the cycle of
victimization and victimhood, retribution and suffering.
—BRYAN STEVENSON, *JUST MERCY*

I found the old photo several days ago while organizing a stack of neglected files. It's a picture of three-year-old me celebrating Easter. My mom kneels on the floor next to me, large curlers covering her head. My Easter basket sits nearby, and I'm holding a colorful pinwheel, my cheeks puffed out as I blow and make it spin. It's a picture of purity, childlike innocence full of possibility and promise.

As I studied the photo these many years later, I looked at the little girl with a heart of compassion. This is a new practice for me. Historically my habit has been a shame-filled one, as I tend to browbeat myself with all the coulda, shoulda, woulda's of years gone by. But this particular day, photo in hand, I felt compassion, a wave of motherly kindness for the little girl who would one day face so many losses.

Bless her. She was so small, innocent. She still believed in dreams come true, didn't yet understand that life can be so very hard.

Perhaps it is the result of my age and the knowledge that my life is likely more than half over, but I feel a bit melancholy as I consider this one life I've lived. If I could travel back in time, I would do so many things differently. I see too many mistakes and missteps, and the regret weighs heavily on me.

But I also see the wrongs done by people I trusted, the ones who snuffed out that little girl's innocence. Because of their own unhealed pain, they caused much of my own. When I look at the girl holding the pinwheel, I see a tangled and complex history that is impossible to fully unravel and understand. Who is responsible? Where did it all go wrong, and how did her heart end up such a tangled mess?

On a sleepless night long ago, Jesus prayed in the garden of Gethsemane on the night before His crucifixion and death. Unlike my three-year-old self, He knew what was coming, the betrayals and denials and abandonment by everyone who earlier that same day claimed to love Him. He knew that before the night was done He would be alone. Of course, He didn't want it that way. He pleaded with Peter, James, and John to help him through: "My soul is overwhelmed with sorrow to the point of death. Stay here and keep watch with me" (Matt. 26:38).

But Peter and the others didn't have the same problem with sleep that Jesus did. Three times, Jesus caught them with their eyes closed. Then a short time later, Jesus was arrested in that very spot, and "all the disciples deserted him and fled" (v. 56).

I've been thinking a lot about this dark night. I've been thinking about Jesus' sleeplessness and His loneliness, the agony and necessity of His suffering. Is there a deeper wound than to be betrayed by someone you love, especially when you need them the most? But I've also been thinking about what happened a handful of days later, on the other side of the crucifixion and resurrection, when Jesus ran into Peter, James, and John again: "On the evening of that first day of the week, when the disciples were together, with the doors locked for fear of the Jewish leaders, Jesus came and stood among them and said, 'Peace be with you!' After he said this, he showed them his hands and side. The disciples were overjoyed when they saw the Lord. Again Jesus said, 'Peace be with you!'" (John 20:19–21).

Three days before, Jesus' closest friends had slept while He wept, fled while He faced arrest, denied Him while Jerusalem denounced Him, and then hid while He hung on a cross. They wounded their Savior as much as did the Roman soldiers who swung the hammers that hit the nails. And yet three days later, Jesus went and found them. These cowardly, fair-weather, tuck-tail-and-run friends who royally failed Him.

Rather than punishment, He offered them peace.

"Peace be with you!" He said.

Twice.

While I can easily waste years nursing a wound, Jesus didn't allow Himself even a couple of days. Instead, He initiated peace to those who had condemned Him as well as those who had crucified Him even while He still hung on a cross: "Father, forgive them, for they do not know what they are doing" (Luke 23:34). Then, three days later, He forgave His closest friends with a gift of peace.

With this tender image of Jesus in mind, I look at the little girl with her pinwheel. No, she had no idea of the losses that would mark her life. My body and soul carry the weight of those wounds. I feel them even as I desperately try to be free of them.

But I also see how, on the cross, Jesus began to heal my wounds through the agony of His own. To those of us stuck in stories we never asked for or wanted, Jesus enters in with a promise: *Peace be with you!* He says.

And so today, when I look at the picture of the three-year-old me, I honor the wounds but also forgive those who caused them. Because I know that when you and I choose to forgive as Jesus did, the locked doors of our sorrow are opened to the healing presence of the Savior.

Peace be with you! He offers. In spite of everything, I receive it.

Five-Minute Faith Builder

Therefore, since we have been justified through faith,
we have peace with God through our Lord Jesus Christ,
through whom we have gained access by faith into this
grace in which we now stand.

—ROMANS 5:1–2

Ephesians 4 says, "And do not grieve the Holy Spirit of God, with whom you were sealed for the day of redemption. Get rid of all bitterness, rage and anger, brawling and slander, along with every form of malice. Be kind and compassionate to one another, forgiving each other, just as in Christ God forgave you" (vv. 30–32). Forgiveness is rarely a one-and-done exercise. Often during my middle of the night musings, I realize I need to say the words again: *God, I forgive them. I'm letting it go one more time. I trust you.* It doesn't take the sting of it away, but it reorients my heart and reminds me of the wisdom and love of my Father. Even if you don't trust the person who hurt you, can you trust your good Father? He's asking you to forgive, for your good and His glory. Take a few minutes, eyes closed and heart open, to tell God about those who have hurt you. Give it all back to Him. Then pray my prayer for yourself. Your peace awaits.

DAY 5

THE HARD WORK OF RECONCILIATION

Forgiveness is an act of the will, and the will can function regardless of the temperature of the heart.
—Corrie ten Boom

I didn't see it coming.

For years I'd poured my whole heart into this relationship, nothing held back. I believed in it, fought for it, sacrificed again and again for it. As my friend Danette tells me, "When you're in a relationship, you leave everything on the court." She's not wrong. This is how I roll.

It didn't matter. Without warning and in a head-spinning span of time, I learned the partnership was over. Finished. No satisfactory explanation, no closure.

Ouch.

Although I was fully committed, it wasn't reciprocated. As a result, I felt devalued, used. And utterly confused. *What happened? What did I do wrong?* Then after my self-flagellation, my questions turned outward. *How could you do this? How could you be so callous to someone you claimed to care about?*

I cycled through these two extremes—and a slew of other big emotions—for days following the breakup. Like a rollercoaster, up one minute and down the next, hopeful one day and defeated the next. And when I wasn't blaming myself for the failure, I was blaming the other party. The result? Exhaustion. And I was no closer to settling the matter than I'd been the week before.

As a writer, I've found it is always a bit tricky when sharing a personal story that involves someone else, especially when the other individual isn't painted in the best light. The point of this story isn't to generate sympathy for me or ire for the person who wronged me. God knows I've played both roles in this story. Instead, it's about normalizing the deep pain of relational breakdown and the equally painful work of reconciliation. I'm guessing you have your own story or two.

You see, unless you and I move into a wilderness cave, live alone, and eat off the land, we will encounter people who fail us. Humans have a perfect track record with imperfect relationships. That means every single relationship you and I invest in will, at some point, deliver disappointment.

The real question is, What will we do with the people who fail us? Reject? Or reconcile?

To reconcile means "to restore to friendship or harmony; settle, resolve."[50] In essence, reconciliation in relationship is bringing something that was in opposition and disagreement into a state of resolution, harmony, or compatibility. I feel rebellion rise up within me when I read these words. I don't want reconciliation. I want justice.

Recently, I reread Jesus' famous Sermon on the Mount in Matthew 5. Filled with some of Jesus' most difficult teachings, it includes guidance on how to handle a relationship that doesn't turn out like you expected it to: "Therefore, if you are offering your gift at the altar and there remember that your brother or sister has something against you, leave your gift there in front of the altar. First go and be reconciled to them; then come and offer your gift. Settle matters quickly" (Matt. 5:23–25).

Whew. That one's a doozy. Not my favorite. I'd prefer a verse or two about stiff punishments for those who behave poorly. Even so, I noticed a note in my Bible in my handwriting, right next to Jesus' difficult teaching: "Valuing people requires sacrifice."

Most of my handwritten entries include the date it was written. This one, though, is missing a date, although it easily could have come from any of the various seasons of my life.

Next to these words I also included one final note: "Blame or forgiveness?"

Author Corrie ten Boom was one of my earliest teachers on forgiveness. While reading *The Hiding Place*, her memoir chronicling her World War II experience in a German concentration camp, I learned about the hard work of reconciliation. After her release from prison and the end of the war, Corrie wrote nine books and spoke in more than sixty countries about God's love and forgiveness. But her message of forgiveness was severely tested when she met a former SS prison guard who had come to know Christ. Recognizing him, she faced a difficult decision: blame or forgiveness?

"Even as the angry vengeful thoughts boiled through me, I saw the sin of them. Jesus Christ had died for this man; was I going to ask for more? Lord Jesus, I prayed, forgive me and help me to forgive him."

But the hard work of reconciliation proved even more difficult than she imagined. Struggling to smile or reach for his extended hand, Corrie turned to the only one powerful enough to bridge the divide she couldn't cross.

"Jesus, I cannot forgive him. Give me your forgiveness," Corrie prayed.

"As I took his hand the most incredible thing happened. From my shoulder along my arm and through my hand a current seemed to pass from me to him, while into my heart sprang a love for this stranger that almost overwhelmed me. And so I discovered that it is not on our forgiveness any more than on our goodness that the world's healing hinges, but on His. When He tells us to love our enemies, He gives, along with the command, the love itself."[51]

On which court do you want to live your life? The court of blame and isolation? Or the court of forgiveness and reconciliation? Don't forget: long before a relationship needed your reconciliation, you needed God's. You remember, don't you? Those times you doubted, questioned, rebelled against, disobeyed, denied, and rejected Him? Me too.

"For if, while we were God's enemies, we were reconciled to him through the death of his Son, how much more, having been reconciled, shall we be saved through his life!" (Rom. 5:10).

Make no mistake: reconciliation is some of the hardest work you will ever do. I'm still in the messy process of that work myself. Fair? Not even close. God reconciled you and me anyway. And when we come up empty, He will give us the love and strength to do the same.

Five-Minute Faith Builder

Therefore, if anyone is in Christ, the new creation has come: The old has gone, the new is here! All this is from God, who reconciled us to himself through Christ and gave us the ministry of reconciliation: that God was reconciling the world to himself in Christ, not counting people's sins against them. And he has committed to us the message of reconciliation. We are therefore Christ's ambassadors, as though God were making his appeal through us.

—2 CORINTHIANS 5:17–20

The hard work of reconciliation first requires us to believe God is at work, even when people and relationships fail. And participating in God's work may involve setting solid boundaries and seeking professional help when the relationship is marked by unhealthy patterns or abuse. The ministry of reconciliation doesn't always mean remaining in a relationship. For nonabuse instances of relational breakdown, the process of reconciliation will still be painful. But refusing reconciliation is painful too. Think of a relationship (or two) that is suffering breakdown. What is your part in the divide? How can you make it right? As Corrie did, ask God to give you both the forgiveness and the love you need to extend your hand. Then commit to taking the next step.

PART 8

THE PRACTICE OF PERSPECTIVE

Suffering, regardless of how big or small, has a way of making us nearsighted. As we discovered in the practice of contentment, pain shrinks our world so that all we can see are the circumstances right in front of us. But the practice of perspective helps us see the world beyond our own. Rather than seeing our story to the exclusion of all others, we start to view our struggle in the context of a bigger story, one that includes the suffering of an entire world. Although the practice of perspective doesn't make our losses any less real or valid, it opens our eyes to a big world in need of rescue and to a God who has given everything to do just that.

┌─────────────┐
│   DAY 1   │
└─────────────┘

RECLAIMING WONDER

Who understands the thrill of seeing the first
bright flowers of spring so clearly as one who has
just lived through the long, hard winter?
—DARLENE DEIBLER ROSE, *EVIDENCE NOT SEEN*

From the deck of the mountain cabin, it looked small enough to fit in the palm of my hand. Maybe the size of a toy soldier or a Matchbox car. As small as it appeared from my vantage point, it was one of Colorado's fifty-eight "fourteeners," the famous list of peaks that rise above fourteen thousand feet altitude in the Rocky Mountain range. This particular peak—Quandary Peak—sits at a strong 14,271 feet and ranks thirteenth out of the fifty-eight. A giant among giants.

Even so, from my comfortable Adirondack chair a short ten-minute drive from the trailhead, it looked inconsequential. Holding my iPhone up to snap a picture, I had to zoom in a bit to ensure it wasn't swallowed up by the forest of pines surrounding it in the photograph. Our family planned to hike it the following day. It wouldn't be easy, but surely not as challenging as some reported. After all, Quandary could sit in the palm of my hand, right?

Twenty-four hours later, my legs told a different story. We did indeed summit Quandary Peak, but it took us roughly four hours to climb the three and a half miles to the top. And we still had another couple of hours to make it back down to the bottom. By the time I returned to my Adirondack chair, we'd hiked about seven hours and covered a mere seven miles.

Every inch of my body hurt. Legs, feet, toes, back, arms, hair follicles. We were exhausted. This time, when I looked at Quandary Peak from a distance, I didn't see it quite the same as before. No matter how small it appeared in my camera view, personal experience taught me it wasn't something to be trifled with. I wouldn't underestimate it again.

There is an old and oft-quoted proverb that speaks of our tendency to underestimate those things with which we are most familiar: "Familiarity breeds contempt." Contempt is a strong word, and it makes me shudder a bit. It means to think something is worthless of consideration, unworthy of regard or attention. Familiarity often brings about that kind of negligent disregard.

For example, those who can walk to their kitchen, grab a glass, and put it under a faucet to fill with running water rarely stop to recognize that roughly 884 million people in the world don't have access to safe drinking water.[52]

Ocean waves hit the shore multiple times per minute—with a range of anywhere from five to fifteen seconds—depending on wind speed, the time the wind has been blowing, and the size of the sea it's blowing over. Even so, those who live by the ocean soon stop hearing it, even though the wave cycles never stop.[53]

While today many will reluctantly drive to doctor's appointments they'd rather skip, half the world's population lacks any access to essential health services, meaning they would give anything to have a skilled doctor to see as well as a way to safely get there.[54]

And yes, those who live with the Rocky Mountains right beyond their front decks sometimes forget both the intimidating magnitude and mystery of them.

Familiarity breeds contempt. Unfortunately, yes.

The same can be said for those who have spent any length of time around the gospel. How many of us have lost the reality of the treasure we've been given?

The book of Mark tells the story of Jesus' return to His hometown. After leaving and launching His ministry, He returns to preach to those who watched Him grow up.

"'Where did this man get these things?' they asked. 'What's this wisdom that has been given him? What are these remarkable miracles he is performing? Isn't this the carpenter? Isn't this Mary's son and the brother of James, Joseph, Judas and Simon? Aren't his sisters here with us?' And they took offense at him. . . . [Jesus] was amazed at their lack of faith" (Mark 6:2–3, 6).

Those closest to Jesus struggled the most to believe Him. Their familiarity with Him made it more difficult to follow Him. But that wasn't Jesus' fault any more than the aches and pains from my hike were the mountain's fault. Quandary sat at the same 14,271 feet the day before and the day after my hike. The problem was in my contempt for the truth of its reality.

The same is true for us. Those of us who cut our teeth on Sunday-school lessons risk growing numb to the wonder of God's presence and salvation. We've received His grace so many times that we fail to recognize how grossly undeserving we are of it. We've long heard about God's unfailing love such that we cease to marvel at being a recipient of it. We drink deeply of the gospel's miracle with zero regard for the millions who have no access to it.

Our familiarity with the good news causes us to show contempt for it.

How do we move from contempt to consideration, from disregard to esteem, from being a people who minimize the miracle of the gospel to becoming individuals who are humbled and awed by its extravagance?

Perhaps it requires getting out of our Adirondack chairs where we view the gospel from a distance and, instead, encountering it. We must experience the impossibility of our distance from God and feel our desperation for rescue. Only then will we marvel at a God who gave His own life to reach us. Not just once but over and over again, so we never forget what we have or what it cost to get us there.

It's not enough to grow up with Jesus. You have to be willing to hike His road with Him. Only then will you and I have the barest inkling of the wonder of the gift we've been given.

Five-Minute Faith Builder

See what great love the Father has lavished on us, that we should be called children of God! And that is what we are!

—1 JOHN 3:1

Read Isaiah 25:6–9, a short description of what is waiting for you and me. This is our view from the top, at the other end of our hike with Jesus. Take a moment to imagine what your life would be like without any belief in God, without any hope of His reality and redemption, without any possibility of an eternity in which all wrongs will be made right and all losses made whole. Imagine that this life is all there is and that when it's done, it's done. Your work and relationships have no meaning, and neither do your successes or sufferings. Every bit of your life is random, meaningless, without purpose or point. Soon your life will be over and your name forgotten. All your efforts will evaporate like snow in summer. It's painful to consider, is it not? And yet that perspective increases the value of what we've been given in Jesus. Allow yourself to be humbled and amazed. Then write a short prayer of wonder at this extraordinary gift.

DAY 2

THE CLASSROOM
OF THE WORLD

*This is what the past is for! Every experience God
gives us, every person He puts in our lives is the perfect
preparation for the future that only He can see.*
—CORRIE TEN BOOM, *THE HIDING PLACE*

I leaned against the leather seat of our airport shuttle and sighed with satisfaction. For the prior three days, my husband and I had enjoyed a brief child-free trip to Cabo San Lucas, Mexico, filled with sunshine, sleep, and conversations without interruptions. Divine.

These getaways don't happen often. Because of the needs of our youngest three children and the demands of our jobs, we rarely get dinner dates, let alone trips for two. Over the last couple of years, we've had a total of three date nights and two overnight trips without children, and on both of those overnight trips my husband ended up with a virus and a raging fever within hours of leaving our house. I wish I were joking.

In the weeks leading up to this trip, I held it in my hands like a butterfly that would break if I held it too tight. I kept waiting for the bottom to fall out, my bubble of excitement to burst. But this time all the pieces came together, and we savored every minute of those three days. By the time we packed up and met the shuttle that would take us back to the airport, I felt happy and content. What a gift. And I was grateful.

But within a short few minutes of that sigh of satisfaction, the shuttle exited the gates of the resort and the view outside my window changed. Whereas seconds before palm trees, ocean views, and gardens galore filled the landscape, now the view outside my window showed extreme poverty and deprivation. Everywhere I looked, I saw decaying single-room dwellings, piles of refuse, starving stray dogs, and adults and children with hungry eyes offering to wash our windows for spare cash.

That's when the pieces came together. When I arrived days before, I'd missed it, all of it. I'd been so wrapped up in conversation in the car that I'd missed the world around me. For three days, we'd sat in lounge chairs by the beach and pool with a mountain behind us. What I didn't know while I'd reclined in privileged comfort is that on the other side of that mountain sat a world of want. Safely cocooned, I couldn't see it. Until the day we drove back home and the view outside my window refused to be ignored. My oversight wasn't intentional, but it significantly skewed my perspective.

Humanity is prone to self-consumption. Although at times we're callous, more often than not we're merely ignorant, blind to the world outside of our own. Like the old idiom, we "can't see the forest for the trees" of our personal experience. Seasons of struggle exacerbate this tendency. While we're preoccupied by circumstances that keep us awake at night, we lose perspective on the world and people around us. When this happens—and it happens to all of us—we must drive ourselves over the mountain of whatever is consuming us. Why? Because a bigger view puts our crisis into perspective.

Context matters. Let's say today you went to work and lost your job. How will you pay your rent? What if you can't find something else that you enjoy doing? What if the pay is less than before? Losing a job is tough; I've been there. And you have every reason to experience sadness over what was lost and fear over what might be next. All are valid responses to a hard circumstance.

But when your pain becomes a pit you can't crawl out of, it might be time to change your perspective, to drive to the other side of the mountain and get a glimpse of the world outside your window. Did you know that the unemployment rate in South Africa is close to 30 percent?[55] And that the worldwide median income hovers right around $9,700 per year? That means if you make around $180 per week (or $30 per day), you are above average.[56] Yes, losing a job is tough, for many reasons. At the same time, when I put myself in the classroom of the world, I see my struggle as part of the shared suffering of humanity. And although it is still difficult, I'm no longer alone.

One of the gifts of my longtime cancer journey is how it has connected me with thousands of others throughout the world who are on similar journeys. Where I am inclined to hole up and host a one-woman pity party, the stories of these brave souls help me to see the world outside my own. Although my suffering remains, the bigger context moderates it, making it bearable. Although I still grieve, I also see fresh ways to be grateful for my variation on suffering. Together, by stepping into each other's worlds, we find comfort, companionship, and much-needed perspective.

A word of caution: This practice of reorientation is an individual work. It is not something to weaponize and prescribe for someone else. To attempt to reorient someone else's perspective is to be the worst of Job's friends, adding shame to their suffering. And it's not a "who has it worse" competition. This isn't an exercise in ranking suffering or finding a worse pain to the neglect of your own.

Instead, it's holding your pain and the pain of others in each of your two hands. Then with a new wisdom, a fresh perspective, and fellow strugglers surrounding you, you might find new strength to walk out your own story.

Five-Minute Faith Builder

When I consider your heavens,
the work of your fingers,
the moon and the stars,
which you have set in place,
what is mankind that you are mindful of them,
human beings that you care for them?

—PSALM 8:3–4

For the next five minutes, contemplate the world outside your window. Consider what today might look like for a thirty-year-old in Malawi, which is ranked fourth lowest in the world in median income. Or consider what today might look like for a thirteen-year-old in China, a country ranked second in sex trafficking. Now imagine what today would look like if you woke up in a different place, in a different generation, and with different circumstances. The point isn't to feel guilt about your reality but to broaden your view so you can see your reality in a greater context. How might the classroom of the world give you fresh strength and wisdom for what you're facing today? Write down whatever God brings to mind. Then pray this prayer:

God, open my eyes. Give me a greater awareness of and empathy for those around the world who suffer. Help me to see what you see and be moved by it. Amen.

$$\boxed{\text{DAY } 3}$$

TREASURES IN DARKNESS

*We keep thinking that the problem is out there, in
the things that scare us: dark nights, dark thoughts,
dark guests, dark emotions. If we could just defend
ourselves better against those things, we think, then surely
we would feel more solid and secure. But of course we
are wrong about that, as experience proves again and
again. The real problem has far less to do with what
is really out there than it does with our resistance to
finding out what is really out there. The suffering comes
from our reluctance to learn to walk in the dark.*
—BARBARA BROWN TAYLOR,
LEARNING TO WALK IN THE DARK

One of the best parts of living thirty minutes outside of the city
in a neighborhood where the houses are widely spread apart is
that we sit well beyond the reach of city lights. Although I could climb
the mountain behind our home and see the distant glow of downtown
Denver to the north and Colorado Springs to the south, the light doesn't

reach us where we are. That means when the sun goes down, our country home is swallowed up in darkness. Like black velvet sprinkled with a million diamonds, the expanse of night sky outside my windows lights up with a vast host of twinkling stars.

Of course, this kind of swallowing darkness comes with its own fears too. I regularly see wildlife outside my office window during the daytime, including elk, coyotes, black bears, bobcats, and the occasional mountain lion. If these animals don't hesitate to prowl during the day, imagine their sinister shenanigans at night. Sometimes I see evidence of their activity in the trash shredded into pieces throughout my yard. I'd hate to see what they could do to me. Let's just say that when my dog barks ferociously at the back door, I take her word for it.

Even so, I thank my lucky stars every day that we landed here. The glorious night sky more than makes up for any wildlife threat. Any fear is swallowed up by fascination, any terror eclipsed by awe. Although caution is appropriate, the awareness of creation's wildness only serves to deepen my appreciation of it. In some ways, the mystery enhances my worship.

In her book *Learning to Walk in the Dark*, Barbara Brown Taylor talks about her determination not only to tolerate the dark but to learn how to embrace it and learn from it. "I have learned things in the dark that I could never have learned in the light, things that have saved my life over and over again, so that there is really only one logical conclusion: I need darkness as much as I need light."[57] She suggests that rather than fear the night and attempt to escape it by going inside, shutting and locking the doors, and turning on all the lights, we treat the dark as a classroom and become a student of the dark just as much as of the light.

God created the world from a black canvas. It was the dark that gave birth to His artistic work: "Now the earth was formless and empty, darkness was over the surface of the deep, and the Spirit of God was hovering over the waters. And God said, 'Let there be light,' and there was light. God saw that the light was good, and he separated the light from the darkness. God called the light 'day,' and the darkness he called 'night.' And there was evening, and there was morning—the first day" (Gen. 1:2–5). What if we could learn to see artistic possibility in our seasons of darkness?

My life has been marked by significant suffering. And although I wish it were otherwise, it continues. Often friends make the connection between Job's hard story and my own as they watch the challenges continue to pile on, one after the other. And yet when I look back, I see not only grief but also the gain. My most treasured moments include the times God shined His light on the darkest days, giving me comfort that could not be explained. When I least expected Him, He showed up. Not the way I imagined, not always the way I wanted. But the darkness of my reality made the light of His presence all the more clear. As the prophet Isaiah said, I discovered "hidden treasures, riches stored in secret places" (Isa. 45:3). Like a black velvet canvas that shows off a sprinkling of a million diamonds.

When you and I practice perspective, choosing to have eyes to see God's presence in the midst of our darkest nights, we discover diamonds in a moonless sky. It's a work only God can do, a gift only God can deliver. And the darker the night, the more beautiful the stars.

"Let there be light," He said.

He did it then. He will do it again.

Five-Minute Faith Builder

I will give you hidden treasures, riches stored in secret places, so that you may know that I am the LORD, the God of Israel, who summons you by name.

—ISAIAH 45:3

In Psalm 139:11–12, the psalmist reveals the secret to overcoming a fear of the dark: "If I say, 'Surely the darkness will hide me and the light become night around me,' even the darkness will not be dark to you; the night will shine like the day, for darkness is as light to you." Our ability to tolerate the dark depends on our confidence in God's authority over and power in the dark. God is light. So although darkness may obscure our view, God sees clearly. He's neither unsure nor afraid. All we need to do is grab His hand and allow Him to lead us through. His perspective is enough. Close your eyes, shutting off all external light. Then picture your Father leading you by the hand. Even if you can't see, He can. Trust Him.

DREAMING OF HEAVEN

We cannot anticipate or desire
what we cannot imagine.
—RANDY ALCORN, HEAVEN

I was sitting outside soaking up the summer sun when my phone buzzed with an incoming text from one of our adult sons.

"Can I come home? I need to come home."

For months, he'd faced numerous challenges. A rigorous college academic load and challenging leadership positions, all exacerbated by a pandemic that wouldn't go away. Then in the middle of all that, one of his most important relationships went south. This is our optimistic child, the one whose glass is always half full. And the one who thrives on relationship. I could sense his discouragement, no matter how brief the text.

"Of course. Always. I'll have your room ready."

I remember doing something similar decades before, when I was a sophomore at a small private Christian college. Although in many ways I thrived, I was still a young nineteen-year-old with a fragile self-image and a desperate desire to be loved. So when a few peers made some thoughtless comments about my appearance, it crushed me. I remember the humiliation and rejection. And I remember lying on the bottom bunk in my dorm room when I made the call to my parents.

Can I come home?

There is a homesickness we feel in places of pain. No matter the size or source, pain shouts, "This is not the way it's supposed to be!" And no matter the friends we call or distractions we employ, the suffering creates an otherness, alienating us from everything familiar. And causing us to long for home with a cry that rattles our bones.

The author of Hebrews recounts the many men and women of faith who experienced this homesickness in suffering: "All these people were still living by faith when they died. They did not receive the things promised; they only saw them and welcomed them from a distance, admitting that they were foreigners and strangers on earth. People who say such things show that they are looking for a country of their own. If they had been thinking of the country they had left, they would have had opportunity to return. Instead, they were longing for a better country—a heavenly one" (Heb. 11:13–16).

Longing for heaven. Homesick. But this kind of homesickness can't be cured by an earthly solution.

In 2014, I got a phone call from my dad while I was speaking at an event in Florida. While I sat in my hotel room thousands of miles away, my dad told me that he had only a few months left to live. Pancreatic cancer is vicious, and my father's was no exception.

That was May 8. By August 19 he was gone. In those three short months, I watched my father process the reality of his mortality. Earlier that same year, I'd received a second cancer diagnosis, so I took notes. I watched him mourn his impending death, the future he'd dreamed of with his wife, children, grandchildren, and friends, the memories we'd make without him, the plans he'd made but wouldn't achieve.

But I also watched him dream of heaven. As if he were planning a once-in-a-lifetime vacation, I saw his anticipation and excitement, and watched as he planned and prepared. He read his Bible more, talked about Jesus more. And although he grieved, he also experienced real joy. After spending his adulthood dreaming of heaven, that dream was about to be fulfilled.

Homesick. He was homesick.

Can I come home?

Of course. Always. I'll have your room ready.

On August 19, 2014, he finally got to see it.

Although you and I have mailing addresses, this is not our home. It will never be our home. We feel the ache of this truth every time the temporary walls of our lives crumble and crash. It is oh so easy to forget that this life is not all there is.

But what if we spent more time dreaming and planning for heaven? What if we allowed ourselves the luxury of anticipation, of dreaming of the life that is to come with as much enthusiasm as we dream of our next tropical vacation? Doing so is part of the practice of perspective, and one of the secrets to a faith that does not fail.

As real as our challenges are, heaven must become even more real. That pain you feel? You're homesick. But that's okay, because to be homesick only confirms that the best is yet to come. Go ahead and dream, even while you weep. One day soon, you will finally be home. And He'll have your room ready.

Five-Minute Faith Builder

But about the resurrection of the dead—have you not read what God said to you, "I am the God of Abraham, the God of Isaac, and the God of Jacob"? He is not the God of the dead but of the living.

—MATTHEW 22:31–32

To begin, read Revelation 21, slowly: "Then I saw 'a new heaven and a new earth,' for the first heaven and the first earth had passed away, and there was no longer any sea. I saw the Holy City, the new Jerusalem, coming down out of heaven from God, prepared as a bride beautifully dressed for her husband. And I heard a loud voice from the throne saying, 'Look! God's dwelling place is now among the people, and he will dwell with them. They will be his people, and God himself will be with them and be their God. "He will wipe every tear from their eyes. There will be no more death" or mourning or crying or pain, for the old order of things has passed away.' He who was seated on the throne said, 'I am making everything new!'" (Rev. 21:1–5).

Next highlight any word or phrase in this selection of Scripture that stirs your spirit or is meaningful to you in some way.

Finally, list the many things you can't wait to experience in heaven. As if you were planning the trip of a lifetime—it is!—imagine what it will be like and allow yourself the joy of anticipation.

DAY 5

KNOWING GOD

*Once you become aware that the main business
that you are here for is to know God, most of life's
problems fall into place of their own accord.*
—J. I. PACKER, *KNOWING GOD*

L et's talk gifts.

Birthday gifts. Christmas gifts. Gifts for teachers, mothers, valentines. And let's not forget the dreaded anniversary gifts, organized by year from year 1 to year 60, which tradition says will grant you prosperity and success in your relationship as long as you get it right. By the way, the recommended gift for year 11 is steel. Good luck with that one.

Regardless of the celebration, gifts add a measure of childlike excitement to the experience, as well as no small amount of stress. If you get the right gift, everything is fantastic. But if you don't? Go ahead and grab yourself a blanket while you head to the couch. You'll be sleeping there tonight.

The secret of good gift-giving is having an intimate knowledge of the recipient. If you know your child's teacher has significant environmental allergies, you might not send her a bouquet of wildflowers. If your sweetheart doesn't like sweets, you won't get him a heart-shaped box of chocolates on Valentine's Day. It all comes down to how well you know the heart of the one you love.

When my lifelong dream of marriage and children ended in divorce and single motherhood at the age of twenty-seven, I felt confident that God didn't care about me. God and I had been in relationship for nearly three decades, a relationship that involved weekly church attendance, regular Bible reading, and plenty of volunteer service. I prayed and praised and obeyed like a champ. In addition, I'd prayed faithfully for my one-day husband and children from the time I was in middle school. It was what I wanted more than anything. Even so, He didn't deliver the one gift I asked Him for, in devastating fashion.

Why, God? I asked more than once.

I didn't get a good answer. Either He didn't really know me or He didn't care about me. The reality of my circumstances plus my conclusions about God's apparent inactivity led me to a strong belief about His character, motives, and heart.

I felt good about my math. After all, the facts are the facts. God's gift-giving left something to be desired.

But what if, after all of our years together, it wasn't so much that He didn't know *me* but that I didn't know Him?

I needed to go back to the facts, reexamine the evidence, and either prove my claim or come up with a new one.

That is what I did. I dug into the Bible searching for evidence of God's character and His affection for His people, including me. I scanned for historical stories and patterns that would help me interpret mine. Maybe then I could make sense of God.

This has been my routine for many years now. Rather than filtering my experiences through my own narrative, I started filtering my experiences through the gospel narrative. This is what I discovered:

The stories of God's people throughout history are filled with suffering. Mine is no exception. Adam and Eve lost their perfect exist-ence in God's garden and then lost both their sons, one to murder and the other for committing the crime. Abraham and Sarah left every-thing familiar to follow God to an unknown country, a journey that was filled with God's promises, but very few answers, at least in their lifetime. Moses was an insecure wanderer, Esther an orphan, Ruth an outcast and widow, Joseph a slave. Shadrach, Meshach, and Abednego worshiped God only to land in a furnace of fire. John the Baptist ended up beheaded, Stephen stoned, Paul imprisoned, the disciples executed, except for John, who was banished to solitary confinement on an island. Even Jesus Himself was tortured and crucified after being abandoned by everyone who claimed to love Him.

Why, God? Each had good reason to ask the question, including Jesus (Matt. 27:46).

And yet in spite of the unanswered questions and unrelieved suf-fering, they followed God to the death, in many cases with peace. Why?

I can only make a single conclusion: Their hope remained in spite of their hardship because they knew Him. *They knew Him.* So even when they didn't understand His behavior, they trusted His character and heart.

- "But I trust in you, Lord; I say, 'You are my God.' My times are in your hands" (Ps. 31:14–15).
- "I run in the path of your commands, for you have broadened my understanding" (Ps. 119:32).
- "Now this is eternal life: that they *know you*, the only true God, and Jesus Christ, whom you have sent" (John 17:3, emphasis mine).

It's good to hope for good gifts. But those good gifts should be defined as good as they filter through the reality of our spiritual existence and not just our physical one. If we process and evaluate everything from our careers to our relationships and even our life span through the filters of eternity and God's reality, even the darkest of losses takes on a different and lighter hue. Not any less hard, but not without hope. But this requires knowing God more than pop culture. Knowing His Word more than news feeds. Knowing the promise of His presence as much as the sting of our pain.

"That's the first orientation for good Sabbath-keeping, the Godward one," author Mark Buchanan says. "It is to practice, mostly through thankfulness, the presence of God until you are utterly convinced of his goodness and sovereignty, until he's bigger, and you find your rest in him alone."[58]

Ultimately, our faith will be strengthened not by a temporary change of circumstances but by a permanent shift in our knowledge of God. In knowing Him, we will discover a comfort that extends beyond our capacity to understand or make sense of our grief. We may never know the answers to our "why" questions, but the "who" question can be answered, once and for all.

Five-Minute Faith Builder

Now this is eternal life: that they know you, the only true God, and Jesus Christ, whom you have sent.

—JOHN 17:3

For the past few years, I've prayed a single-verse prayer many times as a means to gaining a broader understanding about God and who He is: "Open my eyes that I may see wonderful things in your law" (Ps. 119:18). I close my eyes, open my hands palms up, and repeat that verse a couple of times out loud. Then I wait and listen. Whatever God brings to mind, I write down in my journal for further contemplation and meditation. I allow that simple prayer to position me as a student in God's classroom, reminding myself that He is both teacher and subject matter. Today, try a similar practice for your Five-Minute Faith Builder, allowing any misunderstandings you might have about who God is to be corrected at His loving hand.

$$\boxed{\text{PART 9}}$$

THE PRACTICE OF CONNECTION

To see the value God ascribes to relationship we need look no farther than the Trinity. Although the Trinity is a challenging theological concept to grasp, the Bible makes it clear that God is Father, Son, and Spirit, three separate and yet essential and interdependent persons. Though they have distinct roles, they work in tandem to accomplish God's purposes on earth and in heaven. If God Himself embodies the necessity of interdependence and connection, why wouldn't we, His creation, need the same? Although we may deny it or resist it, we are wired for relationship, with God and others. And although suffering may tempt us to pull away, the strengthening of our faith requires us to push in. When we do, we discover fresh courage in the community of others.

$$\boxed{\text{DAY 1}}$$

THE COMFORT OF CONNECTION

I bring you news of a living reality that changes everything.
Jesus has come; Jesus will come. Whatever your own
personal darkness, it has been and will be overcome.
—FLEMING RUTLEDGE, *MEANS OF GRACE*

The email landed in my inbox a few days ago. From someone I've never met—let's call him Mark—I read a story eerily similar to my own. He is a few years older than me, married to Margaret, living in Denver. A couple of years ago, he learned he had squamous cell carcinoma of the tongue, and recently it came back a second time, requiring surgery to remove half of his tongue. Now he's working with a speech therapist to learn how to eat and drink and swallow again. And next week he'll meet with the radiation oncology team to determine next steps.

He's afraid, justifiably so. That's why he reached out. At the end of his email, he asked me a question only someone with a similar story could answer: "Is there any advice, words of wisdom, anything you can pass along that you think might benefit me in this stage of my journey?"

With every word of his email, the memories of my own cancer

journey came back in full focus, the images more acute and real than they'd been moments before. I could feel echoes of my suffering and waves of the old, familiar fear. Although time has passed, the healing continues, physically and emotionally. I am not so far removed that I have forgotten. I doubt I'll ever forget.

But did I have any words of wisdom? Wisdom implies expertise. And although I am a survivor, I'm not sure we ever become experts at suffering.

"I'm not sure I have any words of wisdom or advice," I replied. "My faith in Jesus and belief in His unwavering presence with me carried me through. Many days, I didn't feel His nearness and wondered if He'd abandoned me in my suffering. So I kept a journal. Every day, I wrote the day's date at the top of a single page, and throughout the day I looked for evidence of His goodness and kindness and presence and wrote it down. Some pages were more empty than others. But I now have that journal right here in my office, and I go back and remind myself of God's faithfulness, even through the darkest chapter of my life. He was even more present than I realized.

"He is with you too, Mark. This morning I prayed for you and Margaret, for your strength, your quick and total healing, for your peace and courage through the process. And I prayed for God to make it plain to you that He is with you, even here.

"Thank you for allowing me to sit with you in this season, my friend. This too is evidence of His kindness. Because by sharing this space with you, He is redeeming some of my own losses. He will do the same for you."

And with those last words, I once again recognized God's unparalleled mechanism of redemption: God uses the things we still mourn to deliver the deepest comfort. Not only to someone else but also to us.

It's paradoxical, nonsensical. How could the one thing that has most devastated me become the very thing that heals me? And yet this is exactly what happens. Each time I dare to reach out from the place of my grief to comfort someone else in their own, I find the weight of my suffering lessened. Not all at once, and not forever. But a little at a time until I can once again live.

This is the real miracle.

Paul understood this mystery, this miracle of comfort that comes in the giving of it away: "For just as we share abundantly in the sufferings of Christ, so also our comfort abounds through Christ. If we are distressed, it is for your comfort and salvation; if we are comforted, it is for your comfort, which produces in you patient endurance of the same sufferings we suffer. And our hope for you is firm, because we know that just as you share in our sufferings, so also you share in our comfort" (2 Cor. 1:5–7).

Yes, our sufferings are abundant, at times beyond our capacity to bear. Glory, ours is a God of abundant comfort. But just as an inhalation must be followed by an exhalation, comfort received is only fully realized when comfort is shared.

"Blessed are those who mourn," Jesus said, "for they will be comforted" (Matt. 5:4). With that assurance like breath in our lungs, let us likewise breathe comfort on those who are crying out for it. Comfort starts with Him, but it's multiplied with me and you.

Five-Minute Faith Builder

Praise be to the God and Father of our Lord Jesus Christ, the Father of compassion and the God of all comfort, who comforts us in all our troubles, so that we can comfort those in any trouble with the comfort we ourselves receive from God.

—2 CORINTHIANS 1:3–4

In the many years I've been speaking to groups on the subjects of faith and suffering, I've learned we have an extraordinary capacity to bear up under horrific circumstances as long as we can find both presence and purpose in them. The good news? Our losses aren't wasted in God's hands. "And we know that in all things God works for the good of those who love him, who have been called according to his purpose" (Rom. 8:28). One of my favorite exercises during these events is to lead the audience through a life audit. Today, I want you to do an abbreviated version. Make two lists. On the first, list your regrets and losses. On the second, list how those regrets and losses make you a source of expertise and comfort for someone else. When you're done, read 2 Corinthians 1:3–7 again and give your lists to the God of all comfort.

$$\boxed{\text{DAY 2}}$$

THE GIFT OF CONNECTION

> *In friendship . . . we think we have chosen our peers.*
> *In reality a few years' difference in the dates of our births,*
> *a few more miles between certain houses, the choice*
> *of one university instead of another . . . the accident of*
> *a topic being raised or not raised at a first meeting—*
> *any of these chances might have kept us apart. But, for*
> *a Christian, there are, strictly speaking, no chances.*
> *A secret master of ceremonies has been at work.*
> —C. S. LEWIS, THE FOUR LOVES

It was March 11, 2015, when Bethany sent me her first Facebook message.

A week or two before, at the request of a mutual friend, I'd sent her my book *Undone: A Story of Making Peace with an Unexpected Life.* Knowing our stories, the friend thought Bethany might be encouraged by mine. It took me longer than I planned to send it because I was only a couple of weeks out of the most recent surgery, still covered in radiation burns and sporting a feeding tube and tracheostomy. I was in bad shape and had little to give. But that small effort ended up delivering an extraordinary gift.

Bethany knew a thing or two about extended suffering. A couple of years before we met, she and her family moved from their longtime home in Georgia to Tennessee. Then a week later, she learned she had liposarcoma, a rare cancer. Either a move or a diagnosis was more than enough to handle on its own. But both? It wasn't fair.

But Bethany didn't allow the isolation of her move or her disease to become a desert of connection. Within a short time of moving, she started a Bible study with a few women. She could've isolated and self-protected; instead she reached out and connected. In time, the Bible study grew and dozens of women found community with each other. But it started with one woman's pain and her determination to connect in the middle of it.

By the time I met Bethany online, a couple of years had passed as well as multiple recurrences of liposarcoma. Then the friend asked me to send a book. I did. And on March 11, Bethany sent me a message to let me know she'd received it: "Just want you to know the timing of receiving your book yesterday. It was the day we found out my cancer had returned for the fourth time! Boo! But what a treat to come home and find your book in my mailbox! Started it already and know it's going to be a great encouragement. So as usual, God's timing is perfect! Praying for you in your journey, sister. Press on!"

Only God could orchestrate that kind of timing. I wanted to be hesitant. He wanted me to be obedient. I wrote her back: "I'm so sorry, Bethany. Not the news you wanted to hear! *But* (and that's a big *but*) God is not bound by a doctor's diagnosis. Not in the least! He is not afraid, He is not intimidated. So you go out there and fight and live and be assured that the one who created you knows precisely how to fight for you in the perfect way. He will not let you go!

"Glory is at stake here. Look for it. Search for it like treasure. The way God has shown Himself to me over the past four months takes my breath away. He will do the same for you."

After this initial Facebook interaction, we moved our friendship to text. And for the following six years, we exchanged hundreds of messages. I know because I recently went back and looked. In those years, we both offered comfort and received it, asked questions and answered them, asked for prayer and offered prayers. Like a friendly game of tennis, we took turns, embracing the gift of connection. As a result, we both ended up with a stronger faith.

On Sunday, August 15, 2021, Bethany went home to Jesus. I wept. While my soul celebrated her wholeness, my heart ached with her absence. In the years we knew each other, we never met face to face. And yet our practice of connection breathed life into both of us.

Today I revisited her Facebook profile and read what was her final Facebook post on July 25. "We've fought the good fight haven't we? I don't regret one move. My family is here. We are all doing okay. Heartbroken, as you can imagine, but all in the context of knowing 100 percent that Jesus is our *hope* and that as long as we share that connection, we *will* see each other again, my friends! Always remember He is faithful . . . even if and no matter what! #eyesup."

Even if and no matter what. Eyes up! That was her motto, for herself as much as for the rest of us. God is the source of our hope, the object of our greatest joy. But that hope and joy are fulfilled when we live in connection with each other.

In his book *Free of Charge: Giving and Forgiving in a Culture Stripped of Grace*, Yale professor Miroslav Volf speaks of the incredible worth of connection, especially when facing hardship: "We know it is good to receive, and we have been blessed by receiving not only as children but also as adults. Yet Jesus taught that it is more blessed to give than to receive (Acts 20:35), and part of growing up is learning the art of giving. If we fail to learn this art, we will live unfulfilled lives, and in the end, chains of bondage will replace the bonds that keep our communities together. If we just keep taking or even trading, we will squander ourselves. If we give, we will regain ourselves as fulfilled individuals and flourishing communities."[59]

Resilience requires relationship. In the process of giving, even when we have little to give, we regain a portion of what's been lost. And far more besides—new strength to walk out our tomorrows. Eyes up! Yes. And also arms reaching out.

Five-Minute Faith Builder

Let us hold unswervingly to the hope we profess, for he who promised is faithful. And let us consider how we may spur one another on toward love and good deeds, not giving up meeting together, as some are in the habit of doing, but encouraging one another—and all the more as you see the Day approaching.

—HEBREWS 10:23–25

Do a connection inventory. List your most important relationships and then circle the relationships that strengthen your faith. Do you have friends with whom you share the hope-filled truths as well as the hard questions? Do you have someone you trust who trusts you in return, even if it means stating the harder-to-hear truths along with the easier ones? If your list is short (or nonexistent), spend a few minutes exploring the "why" of your isolation and any action you can take to remedy it. Then ask God to lead you to the individuals and communities that will not only encourage you but strengthen your faith.

$$\boxed{\text{DAY 3}}$$

THE HOLINESS OF COMMUNION

I realized that healing begins with our taking our pain out of its diabolic isolation and seeing that whatever we suffer, we suffer it in communion with all of humanity, and yes, all of creation. In so doing, we become participants in the great battle against the powers of darkness. Our little lives participate in something larger.
—HENRI NOUWEN, *TURN MY MOURNING INTO DANCING*

She came up to me at the end of our women's conference. Soft spoken, petite, silver hair, likely in her early sixties. For the prior two days, I'd been speaking to several hundred women gathered from a multicounty area in the Midwest. After two hard years of canceled in-person gatherings, these women were more than ready to be face to face, in the same space. They were hungry for connection, even more than for the glorious donut wall and chocolate fountain in the lobby. Two years' worth of hard stories simmered under the surface, needing the comfort of community. I tried to make space for their stories. As well as for the chocolate fountain.

While I signed books and hugged new friends between sessions, this woman hovered on the fringe. It wasn't until the end of the last session that she finally dared to step forward, introduce herself, and share her story.

"Thank you for what you shared." She spoke softly, looking around, as if worried someone might overhear. I thanked her for her kind words, and then I waited.

"I appreciate your honesty, being able to say out loud how hard it's been for you, and how you wondered if God had left you." She paused. "Of course, I haven't gone through anything as hard as you have." I doubted this to be true. Clearly whatever had wounded her went deep. This preamble was nothing more than her attempt to muster the courage to say in the day what had been eating her alive at night.

"My son died. He was hit by a car," she said.

Noooooo. What a loss. My heart hurt.

She wasn't finished.

"I was the one driving."

Silence reigned the next couple of moments, both of us carrying the weight of those words—her reliving them, my honoring the cost of them. When she spoke again, she told me it had happened decades before, but she'd rarely spoken of it. For years, not only had she been grieving the loss of her son, she'd also been blaming herself for it.

And then, like the first brightening of dawn's eastern sky, she took a breath and went on.

"I think it's time I started sharing my story," she said, and then exhaled. "You shared your story, and it's helping so many people. Maybe I can do the same."

I will never be able to understand the "why" of some losses. Even if I spent every moment of the rest of my life trying to unravel the reasons and make sense of the senseless, I know the "whys" will remain out of reach. But this I do know: When you and I choose to enter into these sacred spaces, sharing our scars while honoring another's, something otherworldly happens. Something holy.

It's called communion. A table shared by the broken and bleeding. A table of death. But also a table of life.

"By becoming flesh and blood, God reached out a hand from the distance of heaven and touched humankind. Bridging the distance of holiness, he not only became someone we can touch but became the one reaching to touch us. . . . In a world that pulled away from pain, Jesus pushed in. He reached for it, experiencing pain so we would know we're not alone in ours."[60]

The moment Jesus exited heaven and entered human skin as a squalling, flesh-and-blood baby, His incarnation made communion possible. God was now within reach, close enough to touch. But our communion with Him wouldn't be complete until the one who healed became the one who bled. This is what Jesus tried to help the disciples understand at the Last Supper table when He broke the bread and shared the cup. He was offering them eternal communion with God Himself. But at the cost of His life. Life for death, and death for life.

Now, two thousand years later, we celebrate communion with another bread and cup. It's an invitation to remember the unbreakable communion we now have at the cost of Jesus' life. But it's not just for remembering. It's also for living.

The communion table is a shared table, Jesus showed us that. But it was never meant to end with us. Just as we've been the broken sitting at Jesus' table, we can offer communion to the broken needing a seat at ours. But you needn't wait for Sunday. Communion can happen in your neighborhood or school, at your office or front door.

Yes, at a women's conference.

Shared brokenness and shared healing. Communion with Jesus and each other. No table required.

Five-Minute Faith Builder

Whoever claims to love God yet hates a brother or sister is a liar. For whoever does not love their brother and sister, whom they have seen, cannot love God, whom they have not seen.

—1 JOHN 4:20

One simple way to practice creating communion spaces with friends and strangers alike is to learn the art of asking open-ended questions to spark deeper connection. Here are a few of my go-to relationship builders:

- What is your dream?
- Tell me your story.
- What's the hardest part of your life right now?
- What's the best part of your life right now?

Remember, there is only one Healer. Your job isn't to fix or cure but simply to connect. Pay attention and listen. Notice the people right in front of you, acknowledge their existence, tell them they matter, show them you care. Who is one person you can experience communion with this week? Resist the temptation to find an easy choice, like your best friend or your spouse. Instead, consider who God might want you to create a table with. Often God strengthens my faith when I follow Him outside my comfortable circle. After all, that's what He did for me.

$$\boxed{\text{DAY 4}}$$

GIVING OURSELVES AWAY

True healing, of deep connective tissue, takes place in community. Where is God when it hurts? Where God's people are.
—PHILIP YANCEY, *WHAT GOOD IS GOD?*

Last week I had my annual oncology checkup, including a thorough physical exam and scope. By the way, for those of you wondering, I don't recommend the scope. Unless, of course, your idea of a good time is having a few feet of pipe with a handy camera on the end stuck down your nose and throat without anesthesia.

Who's going first? I'll pass.

No matter how much time elapses, no matter how many clean reports I get, the memories of too many years of bad news hit me hard every time I walk through the hospital doors. The fear, the nightmares, the pain and images and remembering. The trauma always surprises me a bit, because although I spend a lot of time coaching on the subject, I still want to believe there is a point when it's done, never to return. I know better.

Last week, I learned that hard lesson again. Trauma doesn't go away. It marks us, like scar tissue that's no longer raw but still tender.

Yet again, I received a clear report. I should not be here, I know this. And I refuse to forget the grave that almost claimed me so I can, likewise, remember the gift of this life I've been given.

But even as I celebrate today's good news, others are receiving devastating news. My youngest son told me yesterday that his bus driver's wife died this week, after receiving a cancer diagnosis only a couple of months ago. Just that fast, she's gone. And the happily married man who drives my kids each day is now a widower, struggling to figure out how to live his remaining years absent the one he'd shared life with the longest.

He is only one of many. I don't have enough fingers and toes to count the messages I've received from fellow strugglers—people with diagnoses, divorces, disillusionment. Wayward children, absent spouses, slipping faith. The list is long and the pain varied, but the grief is the same. I'm not sure why they write to me, except for the fact that my struggle has helped them feel less alone in theirs. What they don't know, couldn't know, is that in writing to me and allowing me to enter into a part of their story, they are part of God's mysterious work to redeem my own.

Years ago I stumbled onto Isaiah 58 and I've never been the same. During the time of the prophet Isaiah, God's people were going through the motions of religion. Although they simulated religious devotion through the practice of fasting, their religion didn't change the way they lived. With a touch of indignant interrogation, God exposes the stark difference between religious performance and a vibrant faith.

"Yet on the day of your fasting, you do as you please and exploit all your workers. Your fasting ends in quarreling and strife, and in striking each other with wicked fists. You cannot fast as you do today and expect your voice to be heard on high. Is this the kind of fast I have chosen, only a day for people to humble themselves? Is it only for bowing one's head like a reed and for lying in sackcloth and ashes?" (Isa. 58:3–5).

Although fasting can be a powerful part of the faith-filled life, religious performance—church attendance, communion services, Bible reading, prayer and fasting—matters little if it doesn't translate to a life that demonstrates God's love and grace. To make it abundantly clear, He tells them exactly what He is looking for:

- "To loose the chains of injustice" (v. 6).
- To "untie the cords of the yoke" (v. 6).
- "And break every yoke" (v. 6).
- "To set the oppressed free" (v. 6).
- "To share your food with the hungry" (v. 7).
- "To provide the poor wanderer with shelter" (v. 7).
- "When you see the naked, to clothe them" (v. 7)
- "Not to turn away from your own flesh and blood" (v. 7).

I have been the person described in each of these lines. I've been the chained, the oppressed, the hungry, the wanderer. I know what it's like to feel naked and exposed, rejected and abandoned. I've been the one desperate and needy, and I likely will be again.

Each time, God entered my story through someone else's faith, giving me what I needed when I didn't deserve it. God wants us to understand that healing isn't found in religious performance or in a perfect record of church attendance and repetitive praying.

Healing comes when we move from being merely the recipient of God's grace to a giver of it:

> And if you spend yourselves in behalf of the hungry
>> and satisfy the needs of the oppressed,
> then your light will rise in the darkness,
>> and your night will become like the noonday.
> The LORD will guide you always;

he will satisfy your needs in a sun-scorched land
    and will strengthen your frame.
You will be like a well-watered garden,
    like a spring whose waters never fail.
Your people will rebuild the ancient ruins
    and will raise up the age-old foundations;
you will be called Repairer of Broken Walls,
    Restorer of Streets with Dwellings.

—Isaiah 58:10–12

Like a bank account that only grows the more you spend, when we offer ourselves to the hungry, God multiplies our offering and we both end up full. It defies logic and all explanation, and yet I've seen Him do it for me again and again.

This is the gift of giving ourselves away. In seeking justice and another's wholeness, we find a measure of our own. It doesn't erase the past or eliminate the pain. But God builds up something new from the ruins of the old. And a faith that was slipping suddenly becomes a faith that is strong.

Five-Minute Faith Builder

Carry each other's burdens, and in this way you will fulfill the law of Christ.

—GALATIANS 6:2

Read Isaiah 58. Then choose two pens or highlighters of different colors. First, highlight anything in those verses that requires you to take some kind of action. For example, "satisfy the needs of the oppressed." Then with the second pen or highlighter, mark what God says He will do for you. For example, "The LORD will guide you always." Ask God to show you at least one action He wants you to take based on what you read. Write it down. Then commit to follow through, and thank Him ahead of time for what He promises to do for you.

$$\boxed{\textbf{DAY 5}}$$

STRANGERS AND FRIENDS

We are not machines that can be repaired through
a series of steps. We are relational beings who are
transformed by the mystery of relationship.
—Dan B. Allender, *The Cry of the Soul*

After several days in middle Tennessee with my job as an executive at a performance coaching company, I was ready to fly home. It was a good week, a productive week, but I could not wait to sleep in my own bed.

But as often happens, my travel didn't go as planned.

By the time I arrived at the airport and made it to my gate, I discovered my flight had been delayed. An hour later, they delayed my flight a second time. Another forty-five minutes later, I boarded and exhaled in relief. Finally, homeward bound.

Alas, it was not to be. For another hour, we sat stranded on the tarmac as the crew double-checked an equipment concern. A worthy delay, and I was grateful. Still, my bed beckoned. When we finally took off, I settled into my window seat relieved that home sat on the other side of a short two-hour flight.

But (you knew it was coming) as we made our approach, the pilot informed us we needed to circle Denver International Airport because of a backup of planes. Another thirty or forty-five minutes, then our descent. Finally.

Except the day yet held a grand finale. The moment we landed and I turned on my cell phone, it lit up with a text from my car service, the one that would pick me up and take me the full-hour drive home. My ride had just been canceled. No explanation, no reason. Just canceled.

As I waited to deplane, I considered a meltdown. It was 8:00 p.m. on a Friday night. I'd spent the prior week working full days. I was tired, cranky, and I just wanted to be home.

But I also knew finding a ride would be difficult. Business and vacation travelers packed the airport. It would take at least another two hours to make it to my front door. If I was lucky.

As I walked through the airport, I pulled up each of my ride-share apps and started searching for a car. The first pass yielded terrible results. An hour wait and a small fortune. I closed the apps, refreshed and tried again, bracing myself for more miserable results.

Instead: "Your driver is five minutes away."

What?! It didn't make sense. I didn't care. I clicked on the ride and headed out to the curb. Two minutes later, I sat in the comfort of my ride-share car. What happened next surprised me most of all.

For the next hour, as my driver made his way toward my home, we shared our stories, first his, then mine. We talked about the various challenges we'd faced, what we were thankful for, what dreams we'd let go of, others we were still hanging on to.

At one point, after I mentioned how important my faith is to me, he asked, "Do you mind me asking what kind of faith you have?"

I didn't. For the next few minutes I told him that I love Jesus. With all my heart. I believe God is real and He sent His Son, Jesus, to give His life for mine, something I definitely didn't deserve and couldn't earn. And in a story filled with too much suffering, it's the only thing that has given me both peace and hope. In spite of everything, I know God loves me. I can't explain it, but I can't deny it either.

Emboldened by my openness, he then shared his faith experience. By the time we pulled up to my house, I'd learned that he was raised in a religious cult, married a Christian woman, as a result left the cult of his youth, and he was slowly trying to discover what real faith is, what the truth is. His journey to know Jesus was still new, and it had been a long road for him, including a painful rejection by family members who didn't understand his new belief in Jesus.

But then, on an ordinary Friday night, he made a last-minute decision to put in a couple of hours of work. And that decision led him to pick up a woman at Denver International Airport. A woman whose plane was delayed twice and who was stranded once. A woman who was never supposed to be in his car in the first place. And a woman who told him about her faith in Jesus.

It's easy for me to assume, in the vast sea that is humanity, that God couldn't possibly see someone like me. I am one of billions. Insignificant, inconsequential, easily swallowed up in the chaos that is our world. How could God care to be concerned with details of an individual's life, like a woman's tough travel day or a young man's new faith journey?

But that night, as thousands went about their lives in the Denver metro area, God connected two strangers who needed to hear each other's stories. It was no coincidence. There were too many pieces and parts that had to come together for this single, one-hour encounter.

I believe God went to all that trouble because He knows this is what we were made for—relationship. Community is our air, as essential as food and water. In relationship with each other, whether strangers or friends, we discover something of God. He becomes personal, kind, and able to transform both inconvenience and tragedy, turning them into a table of shared communion.

Five-Minute Faith Builder

We know that we have passed from death to life,
because we love each other.

—1 JOHN 3:14

Pastor Dietrich Bonhoeffer, who was martyred by the Gestapo during World War II, spent his life advocating for community as an extension of Christ. "We must be ready to allow ourselves to be interrupted by God," he wrote. "We must not assume that our schedule is our own to manage, but allow it to be arranged by God." He lived out that claim to death.[61] As you and I move through each day with our eyes on our agendas, it's easy to miss the people on our paths. Caught up in our inconveniences, we fail to see possible divine orchestration. God's heart is full of tender affection for each one of His children: "Are not two sparrows sold for a penny? Yet not one of them will fall to the ground outside your Father's care. And even the very hairs of your head are all numbered. So don't be afraid; you are worth more than many sparrows" (Matt. 10:29–31). God knows each of us intimately, including the strangers we pass. Don't move so fast you miss the opportunity to practice connection. Today, pray this prayer with me:

Father, how wide and long and high and deep is your love for all
of us! Open my eyes and ears and heart to see the people you put
in my path today. And move the Spirit within me to reach out,
connect, and create communion with whoever you call me to, in
Jesus' name.

PART 10

THE PRACTICE
OF WAITING

Few things challenge our faith in God's presence and provision like an extended season of waiting. We can usually muster our spiritual fortitude for a day or a week. But when a week turns into a month and into a year (or longer), our confidence in God's deliverance dwindles. At that point, we either take matters into our own hands in an attempt to help God out, or we give up on our faith altogether. But if we will dare to trust Him, to trust His character, His wisdom, and His timing, seasons of waiting might prove to be the most fruitful of all. Not only will we witness God do what only He can do, but our faith will be stronger as a result.

GROUNDED

"Wait on the Lord" is a constant refrain in the Psalms, and it is a necessary word, for God often keeps us waiting. He is not in such a hurry as we are, and it is not his way to give more light on the future than we need for action in the present, or to guide us more than one step at a time. When in doubt, do nothing, but continue to wait on God. When action is needed, light will come.

—J. I. PACKER, KNOWING GOD

H ere's what I'd like you to do," she said, determination in her voice. I braced myself.

"Over the next few weeks, I'd like you to stay one hundred percent focused on getting grounded."

Getting *grounded*? What did that mean?!

For the prior half hour, I'd sat on the couch across from my long-time counselor unloading the details of another hard season. Our time together felt a bit like a case of the flu as I spewed up all the confusion and relationship turmoil that seemed to follow me. I expected her to give me homework, something tangible that would deliver immediate results. Like two counseling Tylenol, taken with a full glass of water. "Getting grounded" sounded a bit too fluffy for my taste.

Even so, I trusted her. So I grabbed my journal and pen—always at the ready—and prepped to take copious notes.

"Grounded?" I asked. "Explain."

She did.

"I want you to work on getting grounded. No matter what is happening around you, I want you to get anchored, to dig deep and get an inner sense of security in who you are, regardless of what anyone else says or thinks or does."

It has been years since that conversation, and the assignment continues. With time and practice, I'm more grounded than I've ever been. But I now recognize this is a lifelong assignment, for all of us.

In construction, electrical grounding is necessary for safety. This is how it works.

First, the ground we walk on has negative electrical properties. That means the ground is able to neutralize a positive electrical charge. So when constructing a house and adding an electrical system, a builder will "ground" the electrical system so that any excess electrical energy will be discharged through the ground underneath the house. This is important because lightning, environmental factors, damaged or exposed wiring, or even temporary interruptions in electrical service can cause power surges. Without grounding, the excess electricity might injure people, damage belongings, or even spark a fire.

For a house to be a place of life, its electrical system needs to be anchored to something outside of itself: the ground.

And for faith to withstand the surge of circumstances and storms, it needs to be anchored to something bigger than itself. This is what the Psalms speak of when referring to God as a refuge and fortress.

- "The LORD is my rock, my fortress and my deliverer; my God is my rock, in whom I take refuge, my shield and the horn of my salvation, my stronghold" (Ps. 18:2).
- "In you, LORD, I have taken refuge; let me never be put to shame; deliver me in your righteousness. Turn your ear to me, come quickly to my rescue; be my rock of refuge, a strong fortress to save me" (Ps. 31:1–2).
- "He says, 'Be still, and know that I am God; I will be exalted among the nations, I will be exalted in the earth.' The LORD Almighty is with us; the God of Jacob is our fortress" (Ps. 46:10–11).

This isn't easy to do when the world is falling apart around you. Getting grounded is, as it turns out, a lot of work. Just ask the Israelites.

After the Israelites had been enslaved in Egypt for four hundred years, Pharaoh finally relented and released them. This was good news! For a day or two. And then Pharaoh changed his mind. By the time we get to Exodus 14, the Israelites are in a pickle. In front of them sits the Red Sea, a body of water that's impossible to cross. Behind them, an angry Pharaoh and his equally angry army are closing the distance, determined to recapture their slaves.

A raging Red Sea on one side, a raging army on the other. So what did the Israelites do? They panicked, of course.

"As Pharaoh approached, the Israelites looked up, and there were the Egyptians, marching after them. They were terrified and cried out to the LORD. They said to Moses, 'Was it because there were no graves in Egypt that you brought us to the desert to die?'" (Ex. 14:10–11).

Hello, drama queen. Nice to meet you.

"Moses answered the people, 'Do not be afraid. Stand firm and you will see the deliverance the LORD will bring you today. The Egyptians you see today you will never see again. The LORD will fight for you; you need only to be still'" (vv. 13–14).

"Stand firm" in verse 13 is the word *yasab*, which means "to stand one's ground, confront; to stand before, present oneself, commit oneself."[62] It is less about a lack of physical movement and more about internal security, a confidence in certain deliverance. Which is why, in the next verse, God tells the Israelites to get moving.

"Then the LORD said to Moses, 'Why are you crying out to me? Tell the Israelites to move on'" (v. 15).

Be still! Move on!

Quite the paradox. Which is it?

Both.

Be still, God commanded. He wanted them to get grounded, to stop letting panic create anxiety they were never meant to endure. Yes, the Egyptians were coming. And yes, the Red Sea was raging. But the more important piece of data? "The LORD will fight for you."

Move, He instructed. God had a promised land waiting for them, but it sat on the other side of this crisis. They first needed an unshakeable confidence in His lordship. Then, grounded in that confidence, they needed to move toward His promise.

Chill! Be still! Now move!

That'll preach.

One final note. That word *deliverance*? It's the word *yesuah*, "to save." It's the word from which we get the name Jesus.

Go ahead and let that sink in. Because although we may not face Egyptian armies or Red Sea crossings, we face our fair share of impossible battles.

Even so, our Deliverer is coming.

Five-Minute Faith Builder

I keep my eyes always on the LORD.
With him at my right hand, I will not be shaken.

—PSALM 16:8

Where do you need to get grounded? Where do your heart, mind, and soul feel frantic and fragmented? How will you do the work of getting grounded, even while you wait? Maybe you can start by reading Psalm 16. Then write verse 8 on an index card and carry it with you for a full week. Yes, a week. Memorize it. Every time fear, panic, anxiety, and grief threaten to overwhelm you, remember the Israelites caught between the Red Sea and a raging army and get still. Say the words out loud until you remember the name of your deliverance.

DAY 2

EYE ON THE PRIZE

Hoping is not dreaming. It is not spinning an illusion or fantasy to protect us from our boredom or our pain. It means a confident, alert expectation that God will do what he said he will do. It is imagination put in the harness of faith.
—EUGENE H. PETERSON

It'd been his plan since grade school. As proof, I have a note in my Bible with a pencil-drawn airplane in little-boy script. He drew it for me after a field trip to the Denver Museum of Science and Nature, where he marveled at model airplanes. He wanted to go into the United States Air Force Academy. And he wanted to fly.

For the past twenty-five years, we've lived forty-five minutes from the academy. We know about the stringent requirements, the scant number of applicants who actually get in, the grit needed just to make it through the process, let alone the four-year education. As a mom, part of me wanted to redirect his ambitions toward something less likely to disappoint.

But this was his dream. So we determined to support him in it.

This involved ruthless accountability in his academics. Regular reminders of his goal. Support—financial and otherwise—for his high-school cross-country-team experience, volunteer activities, academic clubs, Civil Air Patrol. Long hours scouring the academy website, helping him navigate forms, tests, essays, health histories and exams, requirements that took months to complete. We repeated the same motto again and again to keep him on track: "Eye on the prize, son. Keep your eye on the prize."

Then in the final year of his application process, my dad, a US Army veteran, died of terminal cancer. And eight weeks after that, I discovered cancer was back for the third time. I tried to stay upbeat, remind my son of his goal, not wanting tough circumstances to derail a dream.

The months while we waited for his academy acceptance moved slowly. I was going through surgery, chemotherapy, and radiation. We were all grieving my dad. And our son was trying to finish his senior year of high school while daily checking the mailbox for Air Force Academy letterhead. It was a tense time, a boy clinging to his dream and his mom afraid she might die.

Then, one April afternoon, my phone rang. My son.

"I didn't make it, Mom. I didn't make it!"

Devastation. That is the only word that comes close to describing the agony I felt when I heard my son crying in my ear. I didn't know what to say.

He'd worked so hard, wanted it so bad. So did I.

I'll never forget that day, our grief and our attempts to make sense of it. Our son was weeks from graduation with no idea what he'd do next. We didn't have a plan B. It was too late for scholarship applications and college campus visits. All of his friends knew exactly what they were going to do. He didn't.

I didn't sleep much that night. My mind raced with all the horrible ways this rejection could ruin him. I tried to pray but didn't know what to say.

The next morning, bleary eyed, I awoke and headed to the kitchen. Soon after, my husband joined me, shoulders heavy with the same weight.

Again we waited for our son, knowing that how he faced this day would provide a clue as to how the rest of his life would play out. Leaders are made in their failures far more than their successes. What would he do? Would he let defeat define him? Or would he let it develop him?

When he entered the kitchen, I braced myself.

"Alright. So I've been on the computer, already emailed a couple people. I won't be going to the academy this year. There's nothing I can do about that. But that doesn't mean I won't be able to try again." And he laid out some ideas for how he could carve a different path to his dream.

Eye on the prize, son. Keep your eye on the prize.

It has now been seven years since that day in the kitchen. In those years, our son graduated from high school, enlisted in the US Air Force, served two years, including an overseas station and deployment, and received multiple awards in his post. In the middle of all that, he did what he said he would do: He reapplied to the United States Air Force Academy, a different man than the one who had applied three years before. And this time he got in.

In May 2022, our son graduated from the United States Air Force Academy, a second lieutenant. Yes, he's going to be a pilot. It wasn't easy, and it wasn't without pain. But he kept his eye on the prize, and this time the dream came true.

Although this is a feel-good story with a happy ending, we all have stories where the hard work didn't pay off and the dream didn't come true. Good outcomes aren't guaranteed, no matter how hard we work toward them. This is the only exception: "But whatever were gains to me I now consider loss for the sake of Christ. What is more, I consider everything a loss because of the surpassing worth of knowing Christ Jesus my Lord, for whose sake I have lost all things. I consider them garbage, that I may gain Christ and be found in him. . . . One thing I do: Forgetting what is behind and straining toward what is ahead, I press on toward the goal to win the prize for which God has called me heavenward in Christ Jesus" (Phil. 3:7–9, 13–14).

Jesus is the one prize that won't disappoint. He is our hope, the unfailing object of our faith. And when we keep our eye on Him, no matter the setbacks, our happy ending remains up ahead. In the meantime, we grieve our losses, mourn our disappointments. But even while we weep, we mustn't forget: there is a higher prize, a greater goal, a dream that will never die, even when we do.

Heaven.

Eye on the prize, friend. Eye on the prize. The waiting will be more than worth it.

Five-Minute Faith Builder

But our citizenship is in heaven. And we eagerly await a Savior from there, the Lord Jesus Christ.

—PHILIPPIANS 3:20

In his letter to the Philippian church, Paul encourages us to view our achievements in light of the greatest prize of all: knowing Jesus. He even goes so far as to call all his many worldly successes nothing but "garbage" compared with what is waiting for him in heaven (v. 8). Hard work and worthy accomplishments aren't bad. But we must put our confidence in the fact that, through Jesus, we are loved and belong to God. Better yet, one day we will finally be with Him forever, and our struggles and disappointments will fade in the light of God's never-ending, never-failing love for us. Read Philippians 3:7–21. In your journal or in the margin, write the words "My home is heaven." Then make a list of all the things you are most looking forward to when that day comes. I'll get you started:

- No more fear!
- Being fully seen and fully loved.
- Laughter.
- Seeing God face to face.
- The uninterrupted assurance of His nearness.

CONFIDENT EXPECTATION

For what we need to know, of course, is not just that
God exists, not just that beyond the steely brightness
of the stars there is a cosmic intelligence of some
kind that keeps the whole show going, but that there
is a God right here in the thick of our day-by-day
lives. . . . That is the miracle that we are really after.
—Frederick Buechner

On September 9, 1965, Admiral James B. Stockdale of the United States Navy ejected from his A-4 Skyhawk over Vietnam after being hit by anti-aircraft fire, severely injuring himself in the process. After capture, he was taken to the Hoa Lo prison and POW camp, the infamous "Hanoi Hilton," where he remained for seven years until his release in 1973. During that time, Admiral Stockdale faced malnourishment, denial of medical care, solitary confinement, and multiple rounds of torture.[63] When asked how he managed to survive such brutal treatment for so many years, Stockdale gave a simple answer: "I never lost faith in the end of the story. I never doubted not only that I would get out, but also that I would prevail in the end and turn the experience into the defining event of my life, which, in retrospect, I would not trade."[64]

When asked about those who didn't make it out, Admiral Stockdale answered, "The optimists," he replied. "Oh, they were the ones who said, 'We're going to be out by Christmas.' And Christmas would come, and Christmas would go. Then they'd say, 'We're going to be out by Easter.' And Easter would come, and Easter would go. And then Thanksgiving, and then it would be Christmas again. And they died of a broken heart. . . . This is a very important lesson. You must never confuse faith that you will prevail in the end—which you can never afford to lose—with the discipline to confront the most brutal facts of your current reality, whatever they might be." This last sentence is what Jim Collins, in his book *Good to Great*, calls the Stockdale Paradox: the ability to maintain confidence in the ultimate outcome while facing the hard truth of today's reality. This isn't only an important business practice but also a necessary faith practice.

Faith, according to Hebrews 11:1, is "confidence in what we hope for and assurance about what we do not see." It is believing that God will show up, and living as if it's already true even while waiting. And it is confidence that God will, one day, right all wrongs and restore all that has been lost, so I have no need to waste time trying to do so myself.

At the same time, faith isn't a blind denial of reality. It doesn't ignore hard facts or pretend things are better than they are. Faith holds current reality and future hope in tandem, knowing both are true.

In the book of Lamentations, the prophet Jeremiah spends significant ink talking about brutal reality. For years, he prophesied about the destruction of Jerusalem. And it happened, as he predicted. The Babylonians invaded, burned God's temple, destroyed the city, and enslaved God's people. All that was left was destruction and loss.

- "How deserted lies the city, once so full of people! How like a widow is she, who once was great among the nations!" (Lam. 1:1).
- "This is why I weep and my eyes overflow with tears. No one is near to comfort me, no one to restore my spirit. My children are destitute because the enemy has prevailed" (1:16).
- "I called to my allies but they betrayed me. My priests and my elders perished in the city while they searched for food to keep themselves alive" (1:19).
- "My eyes fail from weeping, I am in torment within; my heart is poured out on the ground because my people are destroyed, because children and infants faint in the streets of the city" (2:11).
- "He has broken my teeth with gravel; he has trampled me in the dust. I have been deprived of peace; I have forgotten what prosperity is. So I say, 'My splendor is gone and all that I had hoped from the Lord'" (3:16–18).

Jeremiah minces no words when he talks about the devastation. He doesn't hand out smiley stickers or sell "It's all good!" T-shirts. He tells the truth with horrific clarity.

And yet Jeremiah also tempers his sorrow with the object of his greatest hope: "I remember my affliction and my wandering, the bitterness and the gall. I well remember them, and my soul is downcast within me. Yet this I call to mind and therefore I have hope: Because of the Lord's great love we are not consumed, for his compassions never fail. They are new every morning; great is your faithfulness. I say to myself, 'The Lord is my portion; therefore I will wait for him'" (3:19–24).

While Jeremiah sat in his sorrow, he took two definitive actions that impacted the strength of his faith:

- First, he changed his thinking: "Yet this I call to mind" (3:21).
- Second, he changed his speaking: "I say to myself" (3:24).

How we think and speak during our waiting seasons influences the strength of our faith in the middle of it. Although Jeremiah's losses are legit, so are his reasons for hope. If he cataloged his suffering but failed to catalog God's goodness, he would soon sink under the weight of his grief.

Instead, he takes stock of how he thinks and how he speaks. And he reminds himself of a truth that is even more powerful than his suffering: even if he loses everything else, God is faithful. Period.

Habakkuk says something similar in his season of suffering:

> I heard and my heart pounded,
>> my lips quivered at the sound;
> decay crept into my bones,
>> and my legs trembled.
> *Yet I will wait* patiently for the day of calamity
>> to come on the nation invading us.
> Though the fig tree does not bud
>> and there are no grapes on the vines,
> though the olive crop fails
>> and the fields produce no food,
> though there are no sheep in the pen
>> and no cattle in the stalls,
> yet I will rejoice in the Lord,
>> I will be joyful in God my Savior.
>
> The Sovereign Lord is my strength;
>> he makes my feet like the feet of a deer,
>> he enables me to tread on the heights.
>
> —HABAKKUK 3:16–19

Hope in a person—a God whose faithfulness never ends and never fails—that kind of hope is a sure thing. He is more dogged than any difficulty and more determined than even death.

That is confident expectation in the face of brutal reality. Life is hard, but the God of hope wins.

Five-Minute Faith Builder

Be patient, then, brothers and sisters, until the Lord's coming. See how the farmer waits for the land to yield its valuable crop, patiently waiting for the autumn and spring rains. You too, be patient and stand firm, because the Lord's coming is near.

—JAMES 5:7–8

To live with confident expectation means to think and speak as if what we hope for is already true. That said, it's important that our hope is in the right place—in God Himself, rather than in a particular outcome. Take a moment to consider how you think and how you speak about your reality. Although your circumstances may or may not change, what can you be certain of? And how can you think and speak differently as a result of your confidence in the presence and purpose of God? Once you've spent a few moments answering these questions, close with the following prayer:

Father, you know my heart's desire in this situation. Please deliver. That said, my hope is in you more than in the outcome. I am confident that, no matter what happens, you are for me and you are with me. You are my greatest desire. I wait on you.

READY FOR
THE RETURN

*We are not always sure where the horizon is. We would
not know "which end is up" were it not for the
shimmering pathway of light falling on the white sea.
The One who laid earth's foundations and settled its
dimensions knows where the lines are drawn. He gives
all the light we need for trust and for obedience.*
—ELISABETH ELLIOT, *THROUGH GATES OF SPLENDOR*

In 2020, right in the middle of the global shutdown from the
Coronavirus pandemic, my good friend Kathi Lipp published a
book called *Ready for Anything: Preparing Your Heart and Home for
Any Crisis Big or Small.*[65] I still remember when she got the spark of
the idea for this book. After living a lifetime in the San Francisco Bay
Area, she and her husband decided to buy a picturesque house in the
lesser known wine country of California's Eldorado National Forest.
As a new homesteader, she faced things she hadn't faced in the city: fire
danger, snowstorms that shut down their roads, power outages, and the

constant difficulty of finding contractors willing and able to drive to her hollow to make repairs. She realized she needed to have her own plan in the event of a catastrophe, whether big or small.

So for much of 2019, she wrote *Ready for Anything*, a practical preparedness guide for "anyone who falls somewhere between 'I'll just trust God' and stocking a ten-year supply of canned pinto beans in the pantry." Little did she know her words would be prophetic.

Not only did the United States shut down as *Ready for Anything* released, over the months that followed she and her husband faced multiple record-setting snowstorms, water damage, extended power outages, and the Caldor Fire, which burned nearly 300,000 acres and came within a half mile of her beautiful new homestead. All in addition to a global pandemic.

It was a good thing she was ready for anything, because she needed to be, more than once.

As we discovered over the past few years, we were not ready for anything. In March of 2020, one friend told me the story of being down to the final squares of their very last toilet paper roll. Having gone to multiple stores only to find empty shelves, she finally resorted to stealing a partial roll out of the bathroom at her work office.

Another friend told me of ordering fifty pounds of rice, "just in case." Yet another did the same with powdered milk. You never know when you might need fifty pounds of rice or powdered milk. (Except never.) Even as I write, the United States is facing shortages of baby formula and tampons, among other things.

"Be prepared," the Boy Scouts warn. Good idea. Just this morning I reviewed a document from a fire-prevention agency telling me how to get my house ready in the event of one of Colorado's wildfires. Trim dead branches, move flammable substances away from our deck, avoid lighting any fires during windy weather. Sound advice.

But how do you and I live spiritually prepared without letting our readiness turn into anxiety, obsession, or fifty-pound bags of powdered milk?

Jesus didn't avoid talking about His death or the end of the world. He repeatedly warned those who followed Him to get ready. (See Matt. 16:21; 17:22; 20:17–19; Luke 12:35–37; 21:5–36; John 7:33–34; 12:7–8.) Having heard His warnings, the disciples had questions: "As Jesus was sitting on the Mount of Olives, the disciples came to him privately. 'Tell us,' they said, 'when will this happen, and what will be the sign of your coming and of the end of the age?'" (Matt. 24:3).

Can you hear a hint of fear? I imagine all that doom talk left them discombobulated.

For the rest of Matthew 24 and all of Matthew 25, Jesus talked about the things to come. The destruction of the temple. The signs of the end times. The fact that no one knows the day or time except for God Himself. I try to imagine the terror it must've stirred up. Which is why, I believe, Jesus then shared two parables, to help them focus on preparation rather than panic.

The first is the parable of the ten virgins (Matt. 25:1–13), and the second is the parable of the bags of gold (Matt. 25:14–30). In the first, ten virgins with oil lamps await the arrival of a bridegroom. In the second, three servants are entrusted with their master's assets while he goes on an extended trip. In both stories, the bridegroom and the master take longer than expected to return.

But only five of the ten virgins took extra oil for their lamps, ready in case the bridegroom took longer to return. And only two of the three servants put the master's assets to good use, the third choosing to bury the money rather than multiply it. When the bridegroom and the master came back, only those who were ready enjoyed the reward of the relationship.

It is often in the waiting that our faith weakens. We lose steam, forget the object of our affection, grow distracted by the immediate and mundane. And yet our Bridegroom is coming, and He's worth more than any new house, new job, or new romance we could imagine.

Jesus said, "Be dressed ready for service and keep your lamps burning, like servants waiting for their master to return from a wedding banquet, so that when he comes and knocks they can immediately open the door for him. It will be good for those servants whose master finds them watching when he comes" (Luke 12:35–37).

So how do we wait well until Jesus returns? I think the answer lies somewhere between standing on street corners with "The End Is Near!" signs and spending our nights drinking and dancing as if death will never come. Jesus said plainly, "Very truly I tell you, whoever believes in me will do the works I have been doing" (John 14:12).

And what did Jesus do? He served the poor, fed the hungry, comforted the sick, befriended the outcast, advocated for the marginalized, communed with the Father, discipled His followers, and everywhere He went He told men and women, old and young, affluent and poor, religious and atheist, moral and amoral, Jew and gentile about the good news that is God's love and plan of redemption for all humankind.

This is our work each day we awake to breath in our lungs. Ready for anything. Until Jesus comes.

Five-Minute Faith Builder

This is how it will be with whoever stores up things for themselves but is not rich toward God. . . . Be dressed ready for service and keep your lamps burning.

—LUKE 12:21, 35

Peter was present when Jesus told these two parables, and heard Jesus' challenge to be ready. Toward the end of his life, Peter penned a similar warning: "But do not forget this one thing, dear friends: With the Lord a day is like a thousand years, and a thousand years are like a day. The Lord is not slow in keeping his promise, as some understand slowness. Instead he is patient with you, not wanting anyone to perish, but everyone to come to repentance. But the day of the Lord will come like a thief. The heavens will disappear with a roar; the elements will be destroyed by fire, and the earth and everything done in it will be laid bare. Since everything will be destroyed in this way, what kind of people ought you to be? You ought to live holy and godly lives as you look forward to the day of God and speed its coming" (2 Peter 3:8–12). Today, consider your readiness. What does it look like, practically, to be ready for God's return? One way I try to be ready is to keep short accounts. When I make a mistake, I confess it to God and to the person I wronged. When someone hurts me, I work hard to move toward forgiveness. These daily actions help me to stay right with God and make my heart ready for Him. Now it's your turn. Ask God to stir your heart with both anticipation and practical application.

DAY 5

LIVING IN THE IN-BETWEEN

One of the greatest strains in life is the
strain of waiting for God.
—OSWALD CHAMBERS

Today is the Saturday in between.

Some call it Holy Saturday, others Silent Saturday. Yesterday was Good Friday. Tomorrow is Easter. But today I sit in the Saturday in between, that long stretch between death and resurrection, when heaven was silent and all the world could do was wait.

During the dark expanse after Jesus' death, unanswered questions hung in the air. The Savior was, indeed, silenced. To whom do we turn when the one who is supposed to have all the answers stops speaking?

I've spent the better part of this morning considering what it must've been like for the disciples and the other Jesus followers when the one they lived for ended up dead. For three years, they slowly became convinced of His messiahship. Throwing caution to the wind, they put all of their faith eggs in the Jesus basket. Family members called them crazy, friends questioned their sanity, others rejected them outright. Still, they chose to follow this man named Jesus.

It wasn't easy to wrap their minds around the many miracles and wonders they'd seen firsthand. It never is. Demons cast out, illnesses healed, the marginalized welcomed, the dead brought back to life. After three years, their scrapbook of Jesus stories bulged at the seams, the many evidences of His divinity spilling out. Human minds couldn't contain the explanations of heaven-wrought glory.

But then in their favorite garden long after the sun had set, one of their friends approached with a mob. He went up to their Jesus and gave Him a kiss. Having agreed on such a sign ahead of time, mob members took their cue and arrested Jesus while the gaping disciples looked on.

Wait. What?!

Some thought this was the beginning of the revolution that would restore all wrongs to right. Peter grabbed his sword.

Jesus told him to put it away.

Surely this was when He'd call down fire from heaven.

Jesus told them He could, but He would not.

Confused, afraid, they ran.

This is what we do when we don't understand. We run.

This is the Saturday in between. God didn't behave the way we thought He would. Like the disciples, we sit in this place of death, facing an outcome we never expected or wanted.

This is not what I signed up for! I imagine the disciples crying. *He was supposed to save us!* They wail.

True.

He wasn't at all what they expected. He still isn't.

He is more. But before the more, the wait.

The in-between.

The someday but not yet.

I've never been much good at waiting. When I want something, I want it sooner than later. That book I want to write or project I want to complete? I want it to be finished now and flawless the first time. My skills as a leader and coach? I expect them to be fully developed and always effective, without struggle and growth and time. I want my children to be mature and faithful today, and my relationships to be what God designed them to be right now. I want to skip over the uncomfortable process and get to the satisfying results.

But I too easily forget: the struggle now is part of the glory later.

To be human is to wait. We wait to be strong enough to walk. To be old enough to stay up late. To be legally the age to drive a car. We wait for the first date to become a wedding date, a pregnancy to deliver a baby, an interview to become a job, an introduction to become a friend. We wait for appointments, web pages, test results, oven timers, coffee orders, bones to heal, and loved ones to come home. We wait for apologies and justice and forgiveness and romance. We wait, and we wait. And we don't wait very well.

So we fill the in-between with all measure of swords and substitutes, hoping the waiting will be eased by whatever weapon we use to distract.

It never works as well as we hope.

We began this series of ten practices with the practice of lament, and I find it fitting that the practice of waiting brings the ten to a close. "Lament is not our final prayer. It is a prayer in the meantime," pastor Glenn Packiam says.[66] It is what we utter, in both words and silence, when we sit in the Saturday in between. It's the sometimes wordless, often tearful prayer of waiting, sitting neck deep in our struggles while waiting and believing in a future redemption.

This is our prayer in the meantime, while we lament what is and wait for what will be. There is hope, even when all other hope is gone. And that hope is in a love that will not fail, a love big enough to write a story that will make all of our lesser stories pale in comparison, a story written for those who wait.

He is alive. He has come and He is coming. Will He find us waiting with eyes on the ground, caught up in today to the neglect of tomorrow? Or will He find us with eyes on the sky, joy on our faces at the return of our true love?

Five-Minute Faith Builder

But I trust in you, LORD;
I say, "You are my God."
My times are in your hands.

—PSALM 31:14–15

What are you waiting for? An apology, a marriage proposal, a pregnancy test? Or maybe you're waiting for a child to come home, a healing to happen, or a job to open up? As Oswald Chambers soberly said, "One of the greatest strains in life is the strain of waiting for God."[67] Whew. Yes. Been there. Still there. In a sense, every page of this book is about being in a waiting place and learning how to strengthen your faith when you don't know how it will turn out. Let me ask you again: What are you waiting for? Every day we live in the Saturday in between while we wait to go to our true home. Can you trust that He's coming for you? And that when He does, all the lingering unknowns will be resolved once and for all? Write down what you're waiting for. Don't be afraid to give voice to the longings of your heart. Then pray the words of Psalm 31:14–15 aloud, placing them in your Father's hands while you wait.

A FAITH THAT WILL NOT FAIL

Your faith will not fail while God
sustains it; you are not strong enough to fall
away while God is resolved to hold you.
—J. I. PACKER, *KNOWING GOD*

At the beginning of this book, I told you that Jesus offered Peter two extraordinary gifts: "Simon, Simon, Satan has asked to sift all of you as wheat. But I have prayed for you, Simon, that your faith may not fail" (Luke 22:31–32).

A warning. And a promise.

A warning that the life he imagined was about to be turned on its head. Suffering was on the horizon, and Peter needed to be ready for it.

But also a promise. Although Peter's world was about to fall apart, Jesus preemptively prayed that he would have the strength and faith to endure it.

But there was a third gift, hidden at the end of their interaction. Do you see it?

"And when you have turned back, strengthen your brothers" (v. 32).

After the warning and the promise, Jesus gave Peter a mission.

His confidence in and love for Peter were so great that He commissioned him to ministry even knowing he would first fail. Because often the only way to dig out from failure and grief is to give them purpose, a purpose that could come about only as a direct result of the pain.

But the best part of Jesus' mission-giving?

"When."

When you have turned back, Peter. *When.*

When Peter's confidence failed, Jesus' confidence prevailed.

Turns out Jesus was right.

Long after Jesus' resurrection and ascension into heaven, Peter wrote 1 Peter. I've spent a great deal of time in 1 Peter over the past several years, trying to understand the transformation of a man whose faith failed in the garden of Gethsemane but who later served to lead the New Testament church. The man we see in Luke 22 isn't the same man we see in 1 Peter. What accounts for such a radical transformation?

Peter was a man of sharp contrasts. Both confident and a coward (Matt. 14:28–31). Acutely aware of his failings (Luke 5:8) and utterly blind to them (Matt. 26:33). In one moment, he announces that Jesus is "the Messiah, the Son of the living God" (Matt. 16:16), and in the next, he arrogantly rebukes Him (Matt. 16:21–23). Peter was passionate, impulsive, well intentioned, independent, and desperate. When Jesus found him, Peter was a simple fisherman. By the time Jesus was done with him, he was a pillar of faith. Still human, but head over heels for Jesus.

Although parts of Peter's final years remain a mystery, there is strong evidence that he ended up in Rome and, along with Paul, was martyred during Nero's notorious persecution of Christians in 64 AD. According to strong legend, Peter was arrested and sentenced to death by crucifixion. Feeling unworthy to die the same death as his Savior, Peter asked to be crucified upside down. It sounds like him.[68]

"Praise be to the God and Father of our Lord Jesus Christ!" Peter wrote. "In his great mercy he has given us new birth into a living hope through the resurrection of Jesus Christ from the dead, and into an inheritance that can never perish, spoil or fade. This inheritance is kept in heaven for you, who through faith are shielded by God's power until the coming of the salvation that is ready to be revealed in the last time" (1 Peter 1:3–5).

"In his great mercy," Peter said. Yes, exactly. It wasn't merit that saved Peter but mercy.

Two New Testament books to the left of 1 Peter sits the book of Hebrews. And hidden in this book is the definition of faith I return to when I need a reminder: "Now faith is confidence in what we hope for and assurance about what we do not see. This is what the ancients were commended for" (Heb. 11:1–2).

For thirty-eight verses after these first two, the author of Hebrews takes a slow walk through the halls of biblical history, cataloging many men and women who lived by faith long before us. Abel. Enoch. Noah. Abraham. Sarah. Jacob. Joseph. Moses. Rahab. Gideon. David. Samuel. It's an odd collection of flawed and complicated humans. Men and women like Peter, and like you and me.

Beyond those named in chapter 11, many more remain unnamed, their faith no less commendable.

"There were others," the writer remembers, "who were tortured, refusing to be released so that they might gain an even better resurrection. Some faced jeers and flogging, and even chains and imprisonment. They were put to death by stoning; they were sawed in two; they were killed by the sword. They went about in sheepskins and goatskins, destitute, persecuted and mistreated—the world was not worthy of them. They wandered in deserts and mountains, living in caves and in holes in the ground. These were all commended for their faith, yet none of them received what had been promised" (vv. 35–39).

Like me, these others were neither spared the suffering nor given the fulfillment of the promise. Even so, they believed.

When I read the words of Hebrews 11—and I read them often—I find fresh courage for my complicated faith journey. I do not walk alone. I follow in the footsteps of many faithful others, men and women who, like Peter and like me, fought for their faith. With the prayers of Jesus filling their sails, they finished well.

I strain to hear the echo of their voices cheering me on as I try to do the same. I picture these ordinary faithful, transformed by the prayers and presence of their God, lining up alongside my race, urging me to press on. I lean in, needing the encouragement of their stories.

Can you hear them?

"Therefore, since we are surrounded by such a great cloud of witnesses, let us throw off everything that hinders and the sin that so easily entangles. And let us run with perseverance the race marked out for us, fixing our eyes on Jesus, the pioneer and perfecter of faith" (12:1–2).

A warning. A promise. And a mission.

As I sit here with these final pages of *A Faith That Will Not Fail*, I am seven years out from my most recent cancer diagnosis and treatment. It is not lost on me the miracle that is my life. I shouldn't be alive.

In addition, a full year has passed since I started writing this book. More of my race has been run while I've filled these pages. And as I look back and consider too many hard circumstances that remain unresolved, I am haunted by a question.

Do I still believe? After everything, do I still believe what I've written?

Although I do my best to write from a place of authenticity and truth, there remain parts of my story I cannot share. In some ways, the unspoken stories are the most painful ones. They are the slow and chronic deaths that sap my strength. The past year has been no exception. While I explored each of these practices, my faith was tested yet again. And I needed these pages for myself.

It's still too early to know how things will turn out, and this leaves me contemplative and sobered. I'm caught in the limbo of what is and what will be, not knowing the final result. Do I believe God is good, even here? Do I believe He is worth following and believing, without any guarantees of a happy ending? Do I trust Him enough to hang on to Him, even if I lose everything else?

If you hope for a quick answer, you don't yet grasp the extent or cost of suffering.

Michele, Michele, Satan has asked to sift you as wheat.

The enemy of my faith has fought fiercely to wreck me—mind, heart, body, and soul. He fights still. I feel it. A friend reached out a couple of days ago to check on me. I asked her to pray: "Please pray that Jesus would find me faithful." She did and will continue, I know this. But before she prayed for my faith, I believe my Jesus did.

By a sheer miracle of grace, I remain convinced of the good news of the gospel. I believe that God is real, He is good, and He is with me. Even so, I suspect—God help me—the sifting is not yet complete. There are times when I wonder: If Jesus had sat with me at a Passover table and, like he did with Peter, shocked my idealism by warning me that my life would be filled with so much suffering, would I have listened?

I doubt it.

Like Peter, I would've responded with naive arrogance, making promises I was not yet prepared to keep: "Lord, I am ready to go with you to prison and to death" (Luke 22:33).

Only I wasn't. I wasn't ready at all.

Over my years of suffering, spiritual pride and bravado have slowly been put to death by the painful awareness of my fragility. Unlike with Peter, my doubts and denials didn't surface in Gethsemane or while Jesus stood trial. Instead, mine found voice in hospital rooms, counseling offices, and the dark of my own bedroom.

CONCLUSION

So once again, I return to Peter, the one who knows about sifting, doubting, and the Jesus who doesn't always deliver: "Be alert and of sober mind. Your enemy the devil prowls around like a roaring lion looking for someone to devour. Resist him, standing firm in the faith, because you know that the family of believers throughout the world is undergoing the same kind of sufferings. And the God of all grace, who called you to his eternal glory in Christ, after you have suffered a little while, will himself restore you and make you strong, firm and steadfast. To him be the power for ever and ever. Amen" (1 Peter 5:8–11).

Yesterday social media reminded me of a post I wrote seven years ago detailing my fragile physical state, my inability to eat or drink or care for myself in basic ways, and my dark discouragement in that place of horrific physical and spiritual pain. I was a mom with four of my six kids still at home, and a five-foot-seven-inch athletic frame that weighed less than 115 pounds. I had a feeding tube, an unhealed tracheostomy, daily doctor appointments and IV hydration, and a faith that was as fragile as my body.

Even so, this year, I turned fifty-one years old. My hair is 100 percent gray, although you wouldn't know it for the skills of my fantastic hair stylist. There was a time when I didn't think I would live to see my forties. And yet here I am, much to everyone's surprise. The life I live remains riddled with challenges: physical, emotional, relational. I wish I could say it has grown easier over time, but it hasn't. Quite the opposite. Even so, several times a year I travel across the United States speaking to auditoriums filled with men and women who want to believe Jesus is worth believing and following too. Each time, my suffering eases.

A warning. A promise. And a mission.

Although my pain wasn't spared, my faith was. This resurrected faith now enables me to enter in with men and women who, like me, find themselves in dark stories filled with the sounds of fear and failure. Just as the men and women of Hebrews 11 did for me, I now line the paths of their stories and shout of a Savior who loves them and prays for them too.

But it took a faith whose flame almost went out to accomplish it.

In spite of our best attempts to avoid it, pain and suffering will continue. Injustice will thrive unabated. Evil will find new ways to bring pain, disease, and war between countries and within families. Questions will remain unanswered. It is the way of things this side of heaven.

Even after all this time, I can still sometimes forget the eternal stakes in the press of the temporal ones. I must remind myself, as do you, that what is at stake isn't the diagnosis or debt, the relationship you long for or the marriage you couldn't do without, the career or the kid or the dream you've long begged God for.

Don't be fooled: there is a spiritual war being waged right now, one that has the territory of your soul at the center.

"But the one who stands firm to the end will be saved" (Matt. 24:13; Mark 13:13).

Before his death on January 31, 1892, Baptist preacher Charles Haddon Spurgeon served thirty-eight years in ministry in London, England, and preached nearly 3,600 sermons and penned dozens of commentaries, illustrations, and devotionals about his assurance in the gospel.[69] Many mornings, before the sun and my family rise to face a new day, I sit in the old leather chair in my office outside of Denver, Colorado, more than one hundred years later with my Bible, a notebook, and one of Spurgeon's devotional collections. One daily devotion in particular I've highlighted more than once, because it captures my hope as I suffer through the many fears and pains of this life while waiting, eyes on the horizon, for the arrival of the next one:

"The joys of heaven will surely compensate for the sorrows of earth. Hush, my fears! This world is but a narrow span, and thou shalt soon have passed it. Hush, hush, my doubts! Death is but a narrow stream, and thou shalt soon have forded it. Time, how short—eternity, how long! Death, how brief—immortality, how endless! . . . The road is so, so short! I shall soon be there."[70]

Hush, my fears. I shall soon be there.

For now, though, I live weak in body and heart but strong in faith. I am surrounded by a cloud of witnesses, beside and behind. Buoyed by their stories of faith, I ask Jesus to help me live my story well. And I ask Him to help you live yours well too.

A few years ago, when I was still neck deep in the process of healing and learning to live again, I listened to Jill Briscoe, gospel preacher and missionary to troubled youth, speak at a women's conference. If I'd heard her speak before that day, I cannot remember it. But that day, Jill's words marked me, becoming one more voice in the cloud of witnesses reminding me to run my race well. Soon after, I wrote her words inside the cover of my Bible. And I often revisit them when I need to remember.

I leave her words with you, the words that keep pressing me toward the finish and a faith that will not fail: "You go where you're sent. You stay where you're put. And you give it what you've got. Until you're done. All the way home."[71]

A warning. A promise. And a mission.

"To him who is able to keep you from stumbling and to present you before his glorious presence without fault and with great joy—to the only God our Savior be glory, majesty, power and authority, through Jesus Christ our Lord, before all ages, now and forevermore! Amen" (Jude 24–25).

Now to Him who is able.

All the way home, friends. All the way home.

Therefore, since we are surrounded by such a great cloud of witnesses, let us throw off everything that hinders and the sin that so easily entangles. And let us run with perseverance the race marked out for us, fixing our eyes on Jesus, the pioneer and perfecter of faith. For the joy set before him he endured the cross, scorning its shame, and sat down at the right hand of the throne of God. Consider him who endured such opposition from sinners, so that you will not grow weary and lose heart.

—HEBREWS 12:1–3

NOTES

1. For a more detailed account of generational trauma and of my dad's faith journey, as well as my own, my third book, *Relentless: The Unshakeable Presence of a God Who Never Leaves*, captures the complicated and redemptive journey of faith for both of us.

2. John Newton, "Amazing Grace! (How Sweet the Sound)" (1779), Hymnary, https://hymnary.org/text/amazing_grace_how_sweet_the_sound.

3. Jennifer Wilken (@jenniferwilken), "Spiritual disciplines nurture steadfastness," Twitter, October 16, 2022, https://twitter.com/jenniferwilkin/status/1581852538340405249?s=42&t=UlLe20I48LwO8Y0npt1sng.

4. For context, Isaiah's warning here is directed to Ahaz, king of Judah during a time when Syria planned to attack. According to verse 2, "Ahaz and his people were shaken, as the trees of the forest are shaken by the wind." Although Isaiah's warning was directed to Ahaz and his people to address their terror, we can make a similar application in our times of terror and fear.

5. In the first eleven verses of chapter 10, Paul includes an abbreviated recap of Israel's difficult history, including their continued struggle to remain faithful to God despite His visible presence and daily provision. Thus, Paul emphatically warns the Corinthian believers of their vulnerability, regardless of how devout they believe they are. We would do well to consider the same.

6. Timothy Keller, *The Reason for God: Belief in an Age of Skepticism* (New York: Dutton, 2008), 234.

7. Dr. Glenn Packiam, "Five Things to Know about Lament," N. T. Wright Online, March/April 2020, www.ntwrightonline.org/five-things-to-know-about-lament/.

8. Merriam-Webster Dictionary, s.v. "lament," www.merriam-webster.com/dictionary/lament.

9. "Book of Jeremiah," Bible Study Tools, www.biblestudytools.com /jeremiah/.

10. N. T. Wright, "Christianity Offers No Answers about the Coronavirus. It's Not Supposed To," *Time*, March 29, 2020, https://time.com/5808495 /coronavirus-christianity/.

11. Michelle Reyes, "Lament Is a Declaration of Hope," *(in)courage*, May 11, 2022, https://incourage.me/2022/05/lament-is-a-declaration-of-hope.html.

12. Dan B. Allender and Tremper Longman III, *Cry of the Soul: How Our Emotions Reveal Our Deepest Questions about God* (Colorado Springs: NavPress, 2015), x.

13. Philip Yancey, *What Good Is God? In Search of a Faith That Matters* (New York: Hachette, 2010), 26.

14. Wright, "Christianity Offers No Answers about the Coronavirus."

15. "Jesus Laments over Jerusalem," Ligonier Ministries, October 16, 2008, www.ligonier.org/learn/devotionals/jesus-laments-over-jerusalem.

16. Michele Cushatt, *I Am: A Sixty-Day Journey to Knowing Who You Are because of Who He Is* (Grand Rapids: Zondervan, 2017), 66.

17. Michelle Ami Reyes, "Three Ways to Practice Corporate Lament," *Small Steps* (newsletter), February 2022, https://mailchi.mp/20b9c6bb5 cc8/is-lament-a-regular-rhythm-in-your-church?e=02e7d074ad.

18. C. S. Lewis, *The Weight of Glory* (New York: Harper Collins, 1949), 43–44.

19. Scott Sauls, Instagram, August 13, 2022, www.instagram.com/p/ChO IkYRshr-/?utm_source=ig.

20. Charles H. Gabriel, "I Stand Amazed in the Presence" (1905), Hymnary, https://hymnary.org/text/i_stand_amazed_in_the_presence.

21. Mark Buchanan, *The Rest of God: Restoring Your Soul by Restoring Your Sabbath* (Nashville: Thomas Nelson, 2006), 175.

22. Joseph Hamrick, "Something to Consider: Hard Truth: 'I Am Capable to Do This,'" *Herald Banner*, January 17, 2021, https://www.heraldbanner .com/news/lifestyles/something-to-consider-hard-truth-i-am-capable-to -do-this/article_9adbc666-56a5-11eb-9fcd-4360fc865f7e.html.

23. Miroslav Volf, *Exclusion and Embrace: A Theological Exploration of Identity, Otherness, and Reconciliation* (Nashville: Abingdon, 1996), x.

24. Brennan Manning, *Abba's Child: The Cry of the Heart for Intimate Belonging* (Colorado Springs: NavPress, 2015), 25–26.

25. Manning, *Abba's Child*, 26.

26. Andrew Murray, *Humility and Absolute Surrender* (Cedar Lake, MI: ReadaClassic.com, 2010), 11.

27. Brother Lawrence, *The Practice of the Presence of God* (New Kensington, PA: Whitaker House, 1982), 15, 16–17.

28. Dallas Willard, *Hearing God: Developing a Conversational Relationship with God* (Downers Grove, IL: InterVarsity Press, 2012), 53.

29. Murray, *Humility*, 6.

30. "Our Covenant," Maclellan.net, https://maclellan.net/our-covenant.

31. "Our History," Maclellan.net, https://maclellan.net/our-history.

32. Thomas Maclellan, "A Wholehearted Covenant," Renovaré, https://renovare.org/articles/a-wholehearted-covenant.

33. Lawrence, *Practice of the Presence of God*, 21.

34. Lawrence, *Practice of the Presence of God*, 30.

35. Timothy J. Keller, "The Man in the Furnace" (sermon), Daniel: Living by Faith in a Secular World (series), Gospel in Life, May 7, 2000, www.GospelinLife.com.

36. Buchanan, *Rest of God*, 67–68.

37. Warren Baker, Tim Rake, and David Kemp, *Hebrew-Greek Key Word Study Bible, New International Version*, exec. ed. Spiros Zodhiates (Chattanooga, TN: AMG Publishers, 1996), 329.

38. Baker, Rake, and Kemp, *Hebrew-Greek Key Word Study Bible*, 2328.

39. Tony Evans (@drtonyevans), "Forgiveness is not pretending like it didn't happen or it didn't hurt," Twitter, May 2, 2022, www.instagram.com/p/CdD9dceujbX/.

40. Leslie Allen, "Shalom as Wholeness: Embracing the Broad Biblical Message," *Fuller* 9 (2017): 40, https://fullerstudio.fuller.edu/shalom-as-wholeness-embracing-the-broad-biblical-message/.

41. Baker, Rake, and Kemp, *Hebrew-Greek Key Word Study Bible*, 1645.

42. Jamie Arpin-Ricci, *Vulnerable Faith: Missional Living in the Radical Way of St. Patrick* (Orleans, MA: Paraclete, 2015), x.

43. Baker, Rake, and Kemp, *Hebrew-Greek Key Word Study Bible*, 1213.

NOTES

44. Henri J. M. Nouwen, *The Wounded Healer: Ministry in Contemporary Society* (New York: Doubleday, 1972), 21.

45. Watchman Nee, *Sit, Stand, Walk* (Carol Stream, IL: Tyndale, 1977), 2–3.

46. Jer Swigart, "Embodied Shalom: Making Peace in a Divided World," Fuller Studio, n.d., https://fullerstudio.fuller.edu/embodied-shalom -making-peace-in-a-divided-world, accessed September 29, 2022.

47. Swigart, "Embodied Shalom."

48. Bryan Stevenson, *Just Mercy: A Story of Justice and Redemption* (New York: Spiegel and Grau, 2014), 18.

49. Henri J. M. Nouwen, *You Are the Beloved: Daily Meditations for Spiritual Living* (New York: Convergent Books, 2017), February 12.

50. Merriam-Webster Dictionary, s.v. "reconcile," www.merriam-webster .com/dictionary/reconcile.

51. Ten Boom, *Hiding Place*, 215.

52. The latest published information on access to clean water was published in 2019 by WHO and UNICEF, pulling from 2017 data: "Global WASH Fast Facts," Centers for Disease Control and Prevention, last reviewed May 31, 2022, www.cdc.gov/healthywater/global/wash_statistics.html.

53. Stephen Salter, "What Dictates the Frequency of Waves?" Naked Scientists, September 13, 2019, www.thenakedscientists.com/articles /questions/what-dictates-frequency-waves.

54. "World Bank and WHO: Half the World Lacks Access to Essential Health Services," World Health Organization, December 13, 2017, www.who.int/news/item/13-12-2017-world-bank-and-who-half-the -world-lacks-access-to-essential-health-services-100-million-still-pushed -into-extreme-poverty-because-of-health-expenses.

55. "Unemployment by Country 2022," World Population Review, https:// worldpopulationreview.com/country-rankings/unemployment-by -country.

56. Glenn Phelps and Steve Crabtree, "Worldwide, Median Household Income about $10,000," Gallup, December 16, 2013, https://news.gallup .com/poll/166211/worldwide-median-household-income-000.aspx.

57. Barbara Brown Taylor, *Learning to Walk in the Dark* (New York: HarperOne, 2014), 5.

58. Buchanan, *Rest of God*, 71.

59. Miroslav Volf, *Free of Charge: Giving and Forgiving in a Culture Stripped of Grace* (Grand Rapids: Zondervan, 2005), x.

60. Michele Cushatt, *Relentless: The Unshakeable Presence of a God Who Never Leaves* (Grand Rapids: Zondervan, 2019), 123–24.

61. Dietrich Bonhoeffer, *Life Together: The Classic Exploration of Christian Community* (New York: HarperOne, 1954), 99.

62. Baker, Rake, and Kemp, *Hebrew-Greek Key Word Study Bible*, 3656.

63. "Notable Graduates: James B. Stockdale," United States Naval Academy, www.usna.edu/Notables/featured/10stockdale.php.

64. Jim Collins, *Good to Great: Why Some Companies Make the Leap and Others Don't* (New York: HarperBusiness, 2001), 83–87.

65. Kathi Lipp, *Ready for Anything: Preparing Your Heart and Home for Any Crisis Big or Small* (Grand Rapids: Zondervan, 2020).

66. Packiam, "Five Things to Know about Lament."

67. Oswald Chambers, *Hope: A Holy Promise* (Grand Rapids: Discovery House, 2015), 62.

68. Encyclopedia of the Bible, s.v. "Peter, Simon," www.biblegateway.com/resources/encyclopedia-of-the-bible/Simon-Peter.

69. Phillip Ort, "Who Is Charles Haddon Spurgeon?" Spurgeon Center for Biblical Preaching at Midwestern Seminary, June 6, 2018, www.spurgeon.org/resource-library/blog-entries/who-is-charles-haddon-spurgeon/.

70. Charles Spurgeon, "January 29," in *Morning and Evening: A Devotional Classic for Daily Encouragement* (Peabody, MA: Hendrickson, 1991), 58.

71. Jill Briscoe, IF:Gathering 2017, February 7, 2017.